"SWAMPWISE"

OKEFENOKEE JOE

Copyright © 2017 Okefenokee Joe Enterprises.

All rights reserved. No part of this book may be reproduced, stored, or transmitted by any means—whether auditory, graphic, mechanical, or electronic—without written permission of the author, except in the case of brief excerpts used in critical articles and reviews. Unauthorized reproduction of any part of this work is illegal and is punishable by law.

ISBN: 978-0-9973371-0-5 (sc)
ISBN: 978-0-9973371-6-7 (e)

Because of the dynamic nature of the Internet, any web addresses or links contained in this book may have changed since publication and may no longer be valid. The views expressed in this work are solely those of the author and do not necessarily reflect the views of the publisher, and the publisher hereby disclaims any responsibility for them.

Any people depicted in stock imagery provided by Thinkstock are models, and such images are being used for illustrative purposes only.
Certain stock imagery © Thinkstock.

Lulu Publishing Services rev. date: 9/26/2017

I dedicate this writing to the
memory of Swampy & Skeeter
to my five grown sons
and their future on this earth
and to the edification of the
entire civilized world.
~ *Okefenokee Joe*

OTHER WORKS BY OKEFENOKEE JOE
Joe's Special Audio Book Series Entitled
"Swampwise" Secrets, Songs & Stories
from the 'Land of the Tremblin' Earth"
"Snake Hunter Snake Talk"
(Their secret habits, and how to find or avoid them)

More of Okefenokee Joe's CDs, DVDs, etc.)
may be sampled, downloaded
or purchased at:
www. Okefenokeejoe.com

AUTHOR'S NOTE

For almost ten years I lived happily in the Great Okefenokee Swamp located in deep South Eastern Georgia. My closest neighbors were the bear, the deer, the alligators, and all the other native wild animals that lived there in the swamp; Its plants and its creatures became my text book, and experience my teacher.

Every day that went by I was treated to and surrounded by the always beautiful, sometimes amazing and unforgettable scenes, sounds and smells of nature.

My life is now devoted to sharing all that I have learned from the plants and the animals themselves, while living alone and so close to *God* and to *His Earth* in the pristine beauty of the great Okefenokee Swamp.

It is my hope that all who read this book will experience, and absorb as I have, a deeper and more keen perception of nature, and the intricate workings in *God's natural world* around us; That in all of us will be instilled a greater understanding, appreciation, and respect for all that *God* has given us on this earth that *He* and *He* alone has created.

CREDITS

The Author gratefully, and humbly thanks the following for their contributions to this work

EDITING

Mr. Donald L. Berryhill: Noted authority on the ecology of the Okefenokee Swamp, Ga
Mr. John R. Eadie: Former Project Leader of the Okefenokee Wildlife Refuge, Ga
Mrs. Ginger Sanders Dunker: Educator, Aiken County School System, Sc

PHOTOGRAPHS

Bill & Linda Macky
Milton Morris Photography
Wolfgang Obst Productions
Betty Frady
Cover photo by Bill and Linda Macky
Kim Mehaffey Kilgore, Eagle Eye Images

ENDORSEMENTS AND ACKNOWLEDGEMENTS

Professor Whitfield Gibbons, Ga
John R. Eadie, Ga
Donald L. Berryhill, Ga
Ron Eagle Feather Colombe, SD
Don Ramblin' Rhodes

PERSONAL SUPPORT & ENCOURAGEMENT

Bill & Linda Macky and my friends at the Edisto island Serpentarium and Earthquest

Okefenokee Joe/Dick Flood

ABOUT THE AUTHOR

In 1976 Okefenokee Joe became the "Johnny Appleseed" of the Okefenokee Swamp! With his hands-on approach to teaching and his experiential knowledge of wild animals and wilderness survival skills, combined with his earlier showbiz knowledge, he introduced to Georgia a unique and exciting form of "edutainment." He skillfully demonstrated how plants and animals can teach humans various character lessons. Among them are responsibility, patience, teamwork, tolerance, and forgiveness.

In the late 1980s he narrated and hosted several Georgia Public Television documentaries. His Emmy Award-winning *SWAMPWISE* program is still aired on *GPBTV* and *PBS* affiliates four or five times a year. To this day these productions *remain the most requested programs GPBTV has ever produced.*

Picture courtesy of Milton Morris, 2014
Mr. "Swampwise" himself!

Okefenokee Joe has been dubbed "a living Georgia icon" in a book entitled *Georgia Icons* by Ramblin' Don Rhodes of the *Augusta Chronicle*. He is well known throughout the Southeastern U.S. as a "self-proclaimed wild life evangelist." Recently he was inducted into the Georgia Family Entertainer's Hall Of Fame. He was also featured in the center of the front page of the *Wall Street Journal*, and on *Dateline NBC*, *Sports Afield TV Series*, *CNN*, and *ABC*, just to mention a few media outlets.

At the age of 83 under his given name of Dick Flood, he was inducted into the Atlanta Country Music Hall of Fame in November 2015. Check out his many DVDs on YouTube. www.okefenokeejoe.com

ACKNOWLEDGEMENTS

"Okefenokee Joe's book "Swampwise" is a superb collection of personal stories that will stimulate anyone's interest in nature and environmental education. The blend of intrigue and excitement in OK Joe's adventures in the wilds of the Okefenokee Swamp will captivate any audience. From youngsters or city folks to seasoned wildlife biologists already familiar with southern swamps and their ways, anyone will learn something from the adventures of Swampy the Dog, Skeeter the Cat, and Streak the Bobcat. Cameo appearances by Suwannee the German shepherd, Jonas the alligator, and Black Jack, an enormous bear, offer further glimpses into the fascinating behaviors of animals that roam the Okefenokee Swamp. Anyone will be well served who pays heed to Okefenokee Joe's swamp wisdom about loving Nature and learning to live with her."

—Whit Gibbons,
Professor Emeritus of Ecology, University of Georgia/SRL

"It was during his formative years that Okefenokee Joe began to recognize that he possessed the unique skill; the ability to establish a connection, and a relationship with animals of all types. Whether their outer coverings were feathers, fur, scales or shells, Joe can relate. Joe became the *Johnny Appleseed* of the Okefenokee. His connection with animals led to a deeper understanding of the ecological principle of interdependency, and man's reliance upon the living, and non-living components of the environment. Joe has even woven his knowledge of animals into his music. His interpretation of animal behavior can be heard in the lyrics of his songs. An informative and entertaining book for anyone seeking to be a little more Swampwise."

—Donald L. Berryhill,
Noted Authority on the ecology of the Okefenokee Swamp.

"This new book, SWAMPWISE, written by Okefenokee Joe, (AKA Dick Flood), is an excellent example of someone who knows what he is writing about. I have known Okefenokee Joe for more than 40 years, and during the almost 12 years that I was Project Leader at the Okefenokee National Wildlife Refuge. He has wowed crowds in person and on television with his music, and wildlife shows. His excellent book tells the story of his dedication to, and knowledge of the Okefenokee Swamp, it's critters, and the big picture of wildllfe conservation. He is a wonderful performer, and an educator, and his book reflects those attributes!"

—John R. Eadie, Former Project
Leader at the Okefenokee National Wildlife Refuge, Georgia

"Okefenokee Joe now brings to us the accumulated knowledge of a lifetime spent learning. Learning about music, art, life, nature, and the fact that everything that is created is done so with a purpose. And he writes about it with intellegence and wit. As a Native American growing up on the Rosebud Reservation in South Dakota, to me his wisdom is so like my people it is amazing! When you read this book "Swampwise", do so with the willingness to learn what Okefenokee Joe has exhibited all his life, and you will be amazed at what you read.

—Ron Eagle Feather Colombe,
Sicangu Lakota, AKA "The Lakota Poet".

"Okefenokee Joe always pulls a fast one on you. Just when you think "education" is boring, he proves you wrong. He goes into his songs and stories about nature preservation and environmental concerns, and you don't realize how much he is making you aware of what you should do in your life about those environmental decisions, until it dawns on you later. The same goes for his new book "Swampwise". I recommend reading it, and you will see exactly what I mean."

—Don 'Ramblin' Rhodes, Nationally Known Music Journalist & Columnest for the Augusta Chronicle, Augusta, Georgia.

TABLE OF CONTENTS

Chapter 1: The Birth of Okefenokee Joe 1
    Part 1: Goodbye Civilization 1
    Part 2: Livin' Off the Land 5
    Part 3: The Decision 8
    Part 4: Melting Right in 9

Chapter 2: Swampy the Dog 11
    Part 1: Becoming Friends 11
    Part 2: Swampy Earns His Name 15
    Part 3: Swampy Meets Jonas The Alligator 17
    Part 4: Moments to Remember 21
    Part 5: Swampy Is Shot By A Poacher 25
    Part 6: Swampy the Survivor 29
    Part 7: Be a Long Time Forgettin' 32
    Part 8: Swampy's Epilogue 34

Chapter 3: Skeeter the Cat 35
    Part 1: Finding Skeeter 35
    Part 2: Skeeter and the Opossum 38
    Part 3: Who's Afraid of the Lightning? 40
    Part 4: Cats Teach Lessons, Too! 44

Chapter 4: Princess Suwanee 48
    Part 1: Cryin' Wolf 48
    Part 2: Snake Hunting with Suwanee 54
    Part 3: The Dastardly Deed 58

Chapter 5: Streak the Bobcat 63
   Part 1: Making Friends 63
   Part 2: The Learning Process 67
   Part 3: The School Bus Encounter 70
   Part 4: "Kee Yote" The Bobcat 72
   Part 5: Streak Meets Kee Yote 74
   Part 6: Tree Climbing 101 77
   Part 7: Streak Meets the 'Clown of the Forest' 80
   Part 8: Squirrels Teach Lessons Too! 82
   Part 9: Back into the Forest 84

Chapter 6: Right Between the Eyes 87
   Part 1: Enlightening Thoughts 87
   Part 2: The Stranger in the Swamp 91
   Part 3: Teamwork 92

Chapter 7: The American Black Bear 95
   Part 1: Getting to Know the Bears 95
   Part 2: Mating Season 99
   Part 3: Moving the Bears 101
   Part 4: Bears Can't Help It! 105

Chapter 8: Resident Alligators of the Okefenokee 110
   Part 1: The King 110
   Part 2: Blind Suzy 115
   Part 3: Jonas 120
   Part 4: Jonas and the Rattler 123
   Part 5: Alligator Territorial Rights 125
   Part 6: Observations of Alligator Intelligence 127
   Part 7: My Gator Scar 130
   Part 8: Why Do Gators Bellow? 133

Chapter 9: Why Snakes? 136
   Part 1: Overcoming the fear 136
   Part 2: Memories of Camp Carson 141
   Part 3: My First Real Snake Hunt 143

Part 4: American Indian Influence 144
Part 5: Growing Up 146
Part 6: Becoming a Pro With Snakes............................. 147

Chapter 10: "Earth Day Every Day" With the Snakes 151

Chapter 11: Okefenokee Joe's Swampwise Snake Safety Tips.. 160

Chapter 12: Nature's Rules of Conduct............................ 165
Part 1: The Golden Rule of Nature 165
Part 2: Fear versus Anger 170
Part 3: Revenge? No SuchThing! 176

Chapter 13: Movin' On... 179

Chapter 14: Some of Okefenokee Joe's Favorite Swampwise Quotes 186

Chapter 15: Back Of The Book Photos............................. 189

CHAPTER 1
THE BIRTH OF OKEFENOKEE JOE

Part 1: Goodbye Civilization

Men with broken hearts, experiencing utter loneliness and deep despair must strive to survive their nightmare ordeal the best way they can. Some might immediately seek and find a new love to fill those terribly empty mental holes in their lives, caused by the anguish in their heart. We hear about that a lot. Sometimes it works, and sometimes it doesn't work. Others may turn to drugs and alcohol. We often hear about that too. Most of them just end up partying and wasting their life away, as they slowly allow themselves to just disappear down the alley ways of time. I chose to go it alone in the swamps of South Central Florida! And that is where I have chosen to begin my story.

The Everglades National Park is a huge expansion of wild and breathtaking beauty. It covers hundreds of square miles of virtually untamed, uninhabitable, and impenetrable swamp and woodland. It's a paradise for all of our precious native wildlife, and in the Everglades all species of native plants and animals are protected.

That is where I spent most of my time from January to April of 1973. I was right in the middle of a divorce. Two years prior, I had already been through one terrible divorce, in which I lost almost everything, including my four sons that I dearly loved. I could not even visit with them because their mother had taken them way up to Washington, DC, and that was 750 miles from where I lived in Nashville, Tennessee. And now I was losing my fifth son and giving up almost everything I owned again! I was also, for the second time in my life, saying goodbye to the woman I loved.

Show business is partly the reason. I had to be gone often, and I will readily admit to my part of the blame. In both cases though, I did not want the divorce. If for no other reason than the sake of my sons, but to no avail, I desperately wanted to stay and try and work things out. But at the same time something else in my life, equally as hurtful, and maybe even more so was looming in the wind, and in my heart and mind.

Throughout the mid-1950s, on up until the early-1970s, under a different name, I was in the music and entertainment business. I had always earned a pretty decent living for my family. I made sure our bills were paid, and I did my best to show my wife and my kids that I loved them dearly.

But career wise, by now, I was just about burned out on the Nashville scene. Over the past ten years or so, It seemed that no matter what I tried, or how hard I tried to do it, the music business would just slap me in the face in return. I had long since lost what little recognition I had gained, in the late fifties and early sixties, with my regular appearances as one of the two "Country Lads"on the Jimmy Dean CBS TV morning show, and my frequent Saturday night guest spots on the world famous Grand Ole' Opry, and my chart recordings on Monument, and Epic Records. The only sure way to gain it back now was with a hit record.

It takes fame to earn the big bucks, and it had become obvious to me, that no matter how good an entertainer is, fame, and the fortune that goes with it, comes only to the chosen few. Without a decent record contract, and nationwide recognition, I was just another loser, wishfully, and hopefully walking the streets of Nashville.

I was forty one years old, and I didn't know how, but I knew somehow I was going to get over all the loss, and heartbreak. Life moves on, and I knew I must move on with it. So, with a broken heart, a broken life, and broken dreams, I finally left both Nashville, my dismantled career and my utterly disfunctional family life behind me.

Because of my mental turmoil, I had canceled all my remaining show dates across the country, and set up my camp in Florida, south of Homestead Air Force Base, right on the bay. Except for the clothes I was wearing, everything I now owned in this world was piled up in the back seat of my jeep.[1]

A friend at the Air Foce Base base had made me a small canvas tent, and that is what I slept in. A good sharp hunting knife, a cast net, a small camp axe, an ice chest, a set of cooking pots, a cast iron frying pan, a flashlight, a canteen, and a sleeping bag made up the bulk of my camp equipment.

My personal items included a pair of ten inch high leather boots, a pair of moccasins, a toilet kit, a wash cloth, a towel, and some extra clothing. Also, I had several snake boxes, a snake hook, and dozens of cloth snake bags, all of which I kept in the jeep. At that time in my life that was all that I owned.[2]

I still remember that terrible helpless and hopeless feeling. I was like a wounded bear, running aimlessly through the woods, hurting in horible pain, and confusion, not knowing which way to turn!

Having no idea what I was going to do with the rest of my life, I prayed to *God* over and over again, begging him to help me heal my heart and my mind, and just leave the past behind.[3]

I found that one way to help me keep my sanity was to walk the canal banks around Lake Okeechobee, in the sugar cane fields of South Florida, hunting for Florida king snakes! Keeping my mind occupied with the hunt served a great deal to relax and console my confused and lonely state of mind. And the walking. I walked canal bank after canal bank, mile after mile, all thru the sugar cane fields. I did that all day, day after day. That helped a lot because I'd be mighty tired by dark, and sometimes sleep came easy. Until I'd wake up in the middle of a terribelly sad dream!

I remember thinking how ironic it was that something I had so thoroughly enjoyed doing years ago as a child for fun and excitement, now, at middle age, I was doing because of hurt, sadness, and despair![4]

I remember telling a Seminole Indian friend of mine that, "Snakes had helped me to save my sanity!" He laughed, and asked me to come with him next door, so I could tell his brother what I had just told him.

It seems that his brother had been married for about fifteen years to a Seminole woman who was a member of the snake clan! And he laughed like the dickens, when I told him that snakes were saving my sanity! In between chuckles he told me that ever since he got married, snakes had been driving him crazy! We all got a good laugh out of that!

In reality, it was true! Snakes and snake hunting actually did help me greatly to overcome my loss, and save my sanity! My mind was constantly busy with the hunt, and all the walking made me so tired, that I was sometimes able to fall asleep easily at night. But I found a far more effective method of healing my heart, and giving me a much brighter outlook toward the future!

One night, when my mind kept bringing up the bad things, and no matter how tired I was I could not fall asleep, an idea popped into my mind! It seemed as if it had come from nowhere! But I'm quite sure I know where! I began repeating the Lord's Prayer out loud, over and over again. And as I did I tried to concentrate deeply on the true meaning of every word. I found that it would take my mind away from the memories. It would take my mind away from everything! In a very short time it would relax my over active brain long enough to fall into a wonderfully sound and welcome sleep.

Yes, I am totally willing to give credit to *God* Our Father *Almighty*, and my strong belief in Him that helped me to put the past in the past, and eventually just move on.

Notes:

[1] From 1956 until 1973 I had been a moderately successful Nashville based singer/songwriter/entertainer.

"Swampwise"

[2] I was no stranger to camping. As a kid from the age of 8 until I reached 18, I spent eight weeks every summer at a YMCA camp in the mountains of Pennsylvania. Later, three years in the army gave me even more experience at camping. I loved it, and I still do!

[3] The first time I started my life over was when I was adapting to civilian life after leaving the army. The second time was after my first unwanted, untimely, unwelcome, and heartbreaking divorce.

[4] See Chapter 9, "Why Snakes?"

Part 2: Livin' Off the Land

Not far from where I was camped on a small island, I found an old wooden boat. It was lying upside down, and parts of it had long-since rotted away. Since it was on high ground, I thought possibly a snake would be using it for shelter, or because there was plenty of room under there, a striped skunk might have made a home out of it. If that was the case, I knew from experience that I must be ready to jump out of range of its musk glands, should it decide to make use of them![1]

I gently pushed the boat up on its side, and peered under it! I didn't see any skunks, but I did see two huge eastern diamondback rattlesnakes coiled up, and sound asleep! The venom extracting laboratory up in Homestead needed all the venomous snakes it could get, and they paid a decent price for them.

The snakes were not yet aware of me, but they were too close together for me to catch one, without the possibility of being bitten by the other. So, with my snake hook I carefully pulled one of them out from under the boat, and quietly let the boat back down. I quickly but gently pinned the snake's head down, grasped it behind its head, picked it up, and put it in a bag! It had still not awakened! I laid the bag down off to the side, and lifted the boat up again.

By that time the other one had woken up, and it had started to rattle. As I had done with the first one, I pinned it down, and captured it. I put it in the same bag with the first snake, and tied a knot in the bag! Those two snakes were going to bring a few dollars my way, and in a sense I had taken to literally living off the land!

I looked the old boat over, and decided that, with a little patchwork here and there, it would probably float. So I dragged it back to my camp, and with some duct tape, and glue, I made it somewhat "sea worthy"!

Except to occasionally cool off and swim a little, while close to shore, I had not been out in the water very far. But now, I had a boat, and I could go almost anywhere out there in shallow parts of the bay. I cut a young cypress sapling down, shaved the bark off of it, and made a sturdy "push pole" out of it.[2]

One bright and shiny day, with my push pole, and my cast net in the boat, I shoved off into the bay! From shore I had been seeing many floating white markers. I had assumed they were attached to crab traps in the water, but for a month or more I had never seen anyone come to check them. I poled over to one, and pulled it up out of the water. It was a crab trap alright! The bait well was empty which proved that it had not been attended to, and maybe it had been abandoned for sure.

From where I sat I counted twenty more floating white markers bobbing up and down all around me. And I was suddenly struck with an idea! Why not take these traps and bait them up? Maybe I could sell the fresh crabs up town somewhere! I checked a few more traps, and none of them had bait in them. I decided they had been abandoned, and it was time to go into action!

I pulled my cast net from under the middle seat of the boat, and set it beside me. Then I began looking on the top of the water for the telltale ripples that schools of fish make, when they are feeding or moving from place to place. I spent the rest of the morning casting for bait fish, and of course I caught some sizable mullet for my own dinner table.

When I thought I had enough bait, I poled around to all the traps, baited each one up, and put it back into the water! It took up most of the afternoon. That being done, I poled back to shore, got into my jeep, and drove into town. I began visiting restaurants, and talking to owners and cooks about buying blue crabs from me. I was lucky enough to line up three of them that would take two dozen crabs each, from tomorrow's catch! And suddenly I found myself in the crabbing business!

The next morning it wasn't just raining, it was pouring down! But I had traps to check, and orders to fill, so I had to pole my boat in the rain. It took several hours to unload all of the traps. I had taken five empty boxes with me to put the crabs in, and all but one was full. So I had a little more than my quota for the day! But as I sat there soaking wet, after my third attempt at bailing the rain water out of the boat, I was beginning to feel a slightly negative realization. Maybe this was not really the kind of business I wanted to get into.

That feeling was heavily reinforced with disappointment when the first restaurant owner I met with that morning refused to purchase his order. He told me that someone else had already supplied him with all the crabs he would need that day. I got the same result and answer from the next would be client! The third, and only remaining buyer, did take his order, and he paid me for it. But my mind was already made up! I told him that was the last batch he'd get from me. I was out of the crabbing business!

Knowing that I needed to find some way to earn a living, I looked into beekeeping, photography, and even the possibility of building a wildlife attraction in South Florida. Snake hunts were fun, and exciting, but I realized that I could never make a decent, dependable living by hunting snakes.

Notes:

[1] The push pole is used by swampers to push the boat, rather than paddle it, in shallow water.
[2] The striped skunk was fairly common all through Florida. I found quite a few of them while hunting snakes. Luckily I always saw them before they saw me, and was able to move far enough away before they decided to spray!

Part 3: The Decision

I was burned out on the music business, and I wasn't about to go back to Nashville, and try it again. I prayed harder every day to *God*, asking Him to deliver me from my dilemma, and to help me decide what to do with the rest of my life.

The answer finally came to me one morning as I emptied a cast net full of mullet into my cooler. For some reason I just happened to remember a halfhearted job offer that I had received from a friend some months ago!

After leaving Nashville and on my way to south Florida, I had stopped by to see my old friend Jimmy Walker, who was managing the Okefenokee Swamp Park, a famous tourist attraction near Waycross, Georgia. During our conversation I had mentioned the fact that I did not know what to do with the rest of my life. He half-jokingly told me that I could come and work at the park, until I decided my future. The job wouldn't pay much, but it would be steady work.

Even though I was pretty much living off the land, I had several monthly bills that I was obligated to pay. Sixty- five dollars a week, with a take home pay of about forty-nine dollars, would not be enough. So I had declined his offer.

Now, with my cast net in my hands, I was asking myself, "What do you mean sixty- five dollars a week isn't enough? It just might save my sanity! All I would need to do to keep from going crazy is temporarily succumb to my fate, and tell the rest of the world to go fly a kite!" Maybe later in my life we could straighten some things out. But right now I felt I was going through more than I could handle.

I dropped the cast net in the bottom of the boat, and poled back to shore! Then I drove to the nearest telephone booth out on the highway, and called Jimmy! He was taken completely by surprise! He never thought I would take him up on his offer. But he told me to come on up to Waycross, and I could start right away!

That's what I did the very next day! I packed all my worldly belongings into the jeep, and with a cute little dog that had come into my life the night before, I began the long drive north to Georgia.

Part 4: Melting Right in

The great Okefenokee Swamp in southeastern Georgia is not just a filthy hole in the ground with stinking stagnant water filled with mosquitoes and scary things. It's beautiful, healthy, and it's clean. So clean that without boiling or treating with chemicals, its tea-colored water is safe to drink! That is something that now a days can be said about few places, anywhere else on earth![1]

And its not really a swamp! There is a constant southwesterly flow to the water. It is actually the headwaters of the famous Suwanee River that flows into Florida, and the St Marys River which flows to the coast of South Georgia. It covers about seven hundred and fifty square miles, dotted with many small islands, of mostly pristine and beautiful forest land.

In 1974, the year after I moved in, it became the largest designated wilderness area east of the Mississippi River. Every plant and animal living in the swamp became protected by law. And it was my back yard!

As it turned out I ended up happily living there for the better part of the next nine years! In that time, without fully realizing it as it was happening, I would learn to be "Swampwise"! I would even become known by a new name!

It was part of my job at the park to give wildlife lectures several times a day. The park management wanted me to talk about snakes in my lectures. Early on, upon hearing all the negative comments our visitors would make about the snakes we had on exhibit, and how they hated them, I whole heartedly agreed. Maybe I could help to ruin the bad reputation that ignorance has placed upon them.[2]

The park had a loud speaker system set up that covered the entire park area. It was there in case of any emergency. It was also used to announce the times of my lectures. The minute I heard it being announced that *Dick Flood* was about to give a wildlife lecture, I ran over to the boat dock where the microphone was, and I hollered,

"Hey! Don't say that name over the loud speakers!"

At that particular time in my life I did not want to be found! Someone hollered back, "What do you want us to call you?"

I answered, "Anything! Just don't call me Dick Flood!"

Someone said,

"How about Okefenokee Joe?" I agreed to that with,

"Ok! Okefenokee Joe is fine. Just don't call me Dick Flood anymore!"

Life deals! It had dealt me a new home and a new beginning, and that's not all! I didn't realize it at the time, but I would come to love the Okefenokee Swamp. My new home would be on Cowhouse Island. It was an old wooden, single-story cabin with a shingled roof located about one mile from the park entrance, and eight miles from my nearest neighbor.

For the first years, aside from my best friends Swampy the dog, and Skeeter the cat, I would live there alone.[3]

The following chapters are filled with flashbacks that tell my story of my life in the Okefenokee Swamp, and the many lessons I learned from the wild plants and animals themselves!

Notes:

[1] The tannic acid created by the decaying vegetation kills most forms of harmful bacteria. It is also the reason that the water is 'tea colored'. The local folks call it "Black Water."

[2] Whether we like snakes or not, they exist. And Nature needs them in her scheme of things. *God* knows what he is doing. If snakes were not necessary, they would not be around. That being the case, we need and deserve to know more about them than just to be afraid of them.

[3] Chapters 2 & 3 are devoted to the stories of my dog "Swampy", and my calico cat "Skeeter".

CHAPTER 2

SWAMPY THE DOG

Part 1: Becoming Friends

I called him "Dog!" I didn't know what else to call him. What a pitiful sight he was that evening, when he wandered into my camp in the Everglades of South Florida. I could see him by the light of my fire. He was a short legged little mutt, wagging his tail, looking lonesome, and half starved to death. He wasn't a puppy. He was full grown, and someone must have left him behind way out there in the wilderness of the 'Glades'.

He looked mighty sad, hungry, and very much in need of a friend. I felt so sorry for him. I was alone too, and I guess I pretty much knew how he was feeling. I needed a friend too. I suppose it was 'love at first sight', for me, because immediately I made an important decision.

As I handed him the remainder of my supper, which was a delicious ham sandwich and made with my last two slices of bread, I said to him,

"Hey, dog, am I glad to see you. You got here just in time. Do you see that jeep over there?"

I was pointing at my 1973 Volkswagon thing. It wasn't a jeep, but that's what I called it.

I went on, "Everything I own is in the back seat of that jeep. This is my last night in the 'Glades'. I'm all by myself, just like you. I could use a friend. You can come with me tomorrow, if you want to!"

That cute little short legged, dog must have understood every word I said, because early the next morning, when it was time to leave, he was sitting in the front seat of that jeep waiting for me!

It's quite a drive from the Everglades of South Florida, all the way north to Waycross, Georgia. It took us every bit of twelve hours to do it.

It was almost dark when we arrived at our destination, and I'll never forget my first look at that broken down shack on Cow House Island, that was destined to become our home.

Built way back in the forties, it was a typical wood framed South Georgia cracker style house, complete with heart of pine board and batten siding. I noticed that some of the shingles on its roof needed repair, and some needed replacing. And some of its windows were broken.

It had no running water, and no electricity yet. It had few modern conveniences at all. I spotted an 'out house' about forty feet in back of the house. An empty chicken coop, badly in need of repair, stood at about the same distance, on the other side of the house. Inside were two small bedrooms, a kitchen, and a living room, but no bathroom.

I said to my new little partner, "Dog that's our new home, and we are going to love it! Just listen right now to those wonderful springtime sounds of the Southern peepers, the crickets, and the green tree frogs! That's some of my favorite music! Dog, what you are hearing are some of the blessed sounds of freedom! It's *God*'s music!"[1]

I walked the few feet back out to the road, turned around, looked at my little friend again, and said,

"Dog! Come on out here! Look over that way boy!"

I was pointing to the west.

"There are no towns, no people, no civilization, nothing but wilderness for over forty miles! And look over that way, dog!"

I was pointing south, and I said, "Nobody for over fifty miles! Dog, we are home! This is it!"

I could tell that my little friend could feel my enthusiasm; by the way he was wagging his tail, pawing at me, and barking excitedly. Already I was thinking of him as my partner, and I knew I was falling in love with him. I just wished he had a name besides "Dog!"

We unloaded the few belongings that we had brought with us, and settled in for the night. I had a blanket, but no pillow, and no sheets. I didn't even have a bed. The floor was good enough. After all, for the past three or four months I had been sleeping on the ground in a make shift tent. I felt absolutely comfortable, and satisfied with my new situation.

The mosquitoes woke us up quite a bit throughout that first night, and the next day I spent most of my time putting in new windows, and tacking up screens on all the doors and windows. And I gave the house a good sweeping, and dusting.[2]

We had some wonderful times during the next several weeks, just getting acquainted with each other, and me learning my job at the park. Life in the swamp was good. I didn't miss my old life, but I did miss my sons, and I wondered about them often. Other than that things were looking up!

One of the first things I learned about my new four legged little friend was that he loved to talk. I had never known a dog quite like him. When I drove to the park to go to work I left him home. He learned quickly not to follow me, or chase the jeep. When I'd get home from work, for the next half an hour or so he would sit in the kitchen chair and just talk his heart out! The sounds he made were a mixture of whines, and high pitched grunts. I'd never heard a dog talk like that before. It was as if he was trying to tell me all that had happened while I was gone!

Sometimes I'd talk back at him. I'd say things like, "Tell me more!", "What happened then?" or "Are you kidding me?" He'd get even more excited when I did that, and his chatter would get faster and louder! I loved it. I always looked forward to getting home so I could watch him, and listen to him talk to me!

Because he entertained me with so many different serious facial expressions and all of them intense, I believe I enjoyed watching him do that, just as much I did listening to him do it! He was precious. I could tell he was good for my heart. And he and I were fast becoming "swampwise" together!

In the beginning our new home had no indoor plumbing, and no heat or air conditioning. There was no bathroom, commode, and no kitchen sink. Just outside the back door was water spigot. There was a deep well out in back of the house, but it would be a while before the electricity would be hooked up. I hauled my water in from the swamp in plastic gallon jugs. I would heat my bath water over the fire in the fire place. I used an old twenty gallon metal wash tub to bathe in. For my drinking and cooking water, I brought in plastic gallon jugs full of safe drinking water from the park, which was just one mile away. With no plumbing, I cleaned up, and made use of that old 'out house' behind our new home.

Until we got a stove, most of our meals were cooked in the fireplace or on the grill out back. I often made a beef or chicken stew that would last a few days. Sometimes I just ate cereal for supper.

For several months my bed was the floor, and a suitcase was my dining room table. Then one day some kind folks from the Baptist Church in Waycross, drove up in an old Ford pickup truck loaded with many useful, and most welcome goodies!

Thanks to those kind folks, I now had a bed, with sheets, and a pillow. A small kitchen table with two chairs to match it, a couch for the living room, a gas burning kitchen stove, and a small electric refrigerator. I was deeply grateful for all the gifts from those loving and caring church members.

For a good while I got into the habit of going to bed with the sun and getting up with it. That was quite a switch from my old life as an entertainer, but I was loving it!

It was late that first fall before I learned the hard way that it gets just as cold in south Georgia as it does further north. Many a night I was forced to sleep on the floor, next to the fire place. The park finally put a gas heater in the house, and I remember the first time I walked in, after it had been installed. I felt as though I was walking into the Holiday Inn! Oh it felt good![3]

Living as I did greatly humbled me. But my job at the park was a kid's dream come true! All I had to do all day was take care of the animals. And I was gratefully enoying my new way of life.

Notes:

[1] Different species of frogs sing at different times of the year. Spring peepers, are tiny frogs that sing at night in the spring.
[2] Sometimes I had a few choice words for those bothersome biting mosquitoes, and yellow flies. But I knew better than to hate them. As my dear friend Doug Elliot often says,"When mosquitoes are young they are tiny, and they live in the water. Little fish eat them. Bigger fish eat those little fish, and much bigger fish eat the bigger fish, and so on. The next time we sit down to a delicious fish dinner, maybe we could thank a bunch of mosquitoes for getting it all started. All of *God's Creation* on Earth is connected.
[3] Cow House Island is the name of the Island I was living on. I was surrounded by pine plantations, belonging to the state of Georgia, and private lumber companies. For the first year most of my fire wood was pine. Long burning hard wood like oak, and hickory was a scarce and highly valued commodity. Dry pine logs burn much faster, and I was forever waking up to put more wood on the fire.

Part 2: Swampy Earns His Name

Several weeks had gone by, and my little short legged, talkative friend's name was still "Dog." I just did not know what else to call him. Until one night I heard him yelp! I quickly jumped out of bed, put on my headlamp, turned it on, grabbed my twelve gauge shotgun, and ran outside!

I found Swampy! He was sitting in the middle of a mud puddle, soaking wet, and filthy dirty. He looked so pitiful. He was not even wagging his tail. Poor thing, he was making that frantic, high-pitched yelping sound that dogs make when they are in pain! He was looking up at me, and by the light of my head lamp, I could see what had happened! And it frightened me!

His nose had swelled up almost as big as a balloon. He looked like Snoopy sitting there! It was obvious that he had been bitten by a venomous snake.

Almost hysterically, I yelled, "Swampy! What kind of a swamp dog are you? You've been snake bitten! Swamp dogs don't let that happen! Swampy, they just don't do that!"

Then I realized what I had done! Without even thinking I had solved a several-week-old dilemma! 'Dog's' name was no longer 'Dog!' He had a name now! A name I had just given him! His name was "Swampy"! And oh how I came to love that cute little short-legged Swampy the dog! He and I had so many wonderful, happy adventures together on Cowhouse Island in the Okefenokee Swamp, because thank *God* Swampy lived through that snakebite![1]

It was about ten-thirty p.m. when that happened. The Veterinarian would not be in his office, but I knew where he lived. I gently put Swampy in the jeep beside me, and drove as fast as I could to the vet's house! We had no phone, so I could not call ahead to make any preparations.

When I knocked on his door and the vet opened it, he took one look at Swampy, and without hesitation said, "Bring him in!"

He placed Swampy on a table, and with a sharp instrument began poking holes in Swampy's face in the area of the snake's fang marks. He gently proceeded to squeeze those areas in hopes that by making the blood flow more freely so that it would force some of the venom out. Swampy did not make a sound through the whole procedure.

He gave him several shots to neutralize the venom, some antibiotic and pain-killing medicine, and reassured me that thank *God*, he would most certainly survive.

I was to take him home, and keep him quiet for a few days. And that is what I did. It didn't take long 'til the swelling and the pain were gone, and he was back to being his old talkative self again.

But there was something brand new, and wonderfully different about him now. His name was no longer 'Dog'! He had a name now! For the rest of his short life he would be known as "Swampy"!

And he turned out to be my best friend and companion in the Okefenokee Swamp!

Notes:

[1] Although it can be a painful ordeal for both the dog and its owner, most dogs survive the bites of our native venomous snakes.

Picture courtesy of Betty Frady
The Dreaded & Deadly Eastern Cottonmouth

Part 3: Swampy Meets Jonas The Alligator

It was my day off! And it was a very special day for me. I had been planning it for several weeks. According to the August tide chart, low tide at Clam Creek on Jekyl Island would be around twelve o'clock noon. That made it a perfect day for us to do what we planned to do. Except for one thing! And that one thing was the weather.

At six-thirty a.m., I was awakened by my alarm clock radio. Tammy Wynette was singing "Stand by Your Man" on the Big Ape Radio station out of Jacksonville, Florida.

I got up, put the coffee on, and walked outside to see what the weather was doing. It was still raining. It had been raining off and on for five days. The ditches near my house were overflowing. There was water all the way up to my front steps. I had hoped it would let up during the night, but it hadn't. On my way back into the house, feeling disappointed, in a disheartened tone of voice I said to Swampy,

"Swampy, it looks as if we will have to find something else to do today. It's still raining out there."

I sat down at the kitchen table with my first cup of coffee, and stared out the window at the pouring rain. I sat there wondering to myself, what else could I do with today? Then I remembered the big cardboard box I had been storing under the kitchen table. In that box was an assortment of unfinished, "things to do" items. Among them were my clay ash trays.

For several months now, in an attempt to earn extra money, I had been modeling ash trays out of clay. I made the ash trays in the shape of a pond. In the pond, or alongside of it, I would create a swamp scene. For example, one of my favorites was a hollow cypress stump with a hole in it. Peering out of the hole was a cute little raccoon. Another was two alligators lazing away on the edge of the pond. Still another was an American black bear bathing in the middle of the pond. My best one though was an action scene of a mother bear protecting her two little cubs from an alligator!

I would take my clay "masterpieces" up town to the middle school, where I was given permission to fire them in the school's kiln. They sold very well in the gift shop at the park for twenty-five dollars.

After breakfast, I began putting newspapers on the table, getting ready to work with the clay, and lo and behold, it stopped raining. I walked out on the front porch to get a better look. The sky was clearing, the clouds were moving westward, and I could see the sun trying to break through!

I saw a pair of crows flying over. They were flying in the same direction as the clouds were moving, and as they passed overhead I heard both of them cawing, as if to say, "It's over! It's over!"

I thought to myself, "They just might be telling the truth this time! It just might clear up!"

Anxiously watching the sky, I stood there awhile, and I began to get excited again. Deciding to take the chance that the weather would definitely clear, I yelled to Swampy, "Swampy, it looks as if we can go after all!"

I had already packed the 'jeep' the night before with the crab net, cast nets, cooler, buckets, and everything else we would need, except for the gallon jug of ice, and the crab bait, which was still in the freezer.[1]

Walking out back to the freezer to get those two things I suddenly heard Swampy begin barking furiously, out in front of the house. I could tell from the way he was barking that there was something really serious going on! As I was running around the side of the house, I could see Swampy with his hair bristling. He was viciously baring his teeth, barking and growling savagely, but I could not yet see what had so violently grabbed his attention!

Finally I was in front of the house, and what I saw put me in dire fear for Swampy's life! A huge alligator was in our yard! It had swum up out of the swamp by way of the overflowing ditches, and it was right at our front door steps! What a monster it was! It was every bit of ten feet long, and with its toothy mouth wide open, it was hissing and blowing at Swampy![2]

Swampy was standing his ground, between the gator and our front steps! He was barking his head off, and snarling at that huge cold blooded, and threatening creature! I screamed at the top of my lungs, "Swampy, Get back! Get away from that thing!" But Swampy continued to stand his ground!

I screamed even louder this time. "That alligator can move faster than you can! He'll have you in his jaws quicker than lightning! Get back! Get away from him!"[3]

The gator opened his jaws wider, and in a jerking fashion, raised the front portion of its body off the ground, as if to lunge at

Swampy! Swampy jumped backwards a few feet, still growling at the gator! But he did not run! He stood his ground!

During this whole scenario I had been hollering, "Swampy, get away from that alligator!"

The huge beast made another 'halfhearted' lunge at Swampy! Then it suddenly turned completely around, and began to swim back towards the swamp. Swampy, taking full advantage of this maneuver was hot on the gator's trail, barking and biting at its tail! The gator swung around, facing Swampy once again, as if to ward him off!

Again Swampy jumped back a short distance! The gator then swung back around, and proceeded to swim toward the swamp. Swampy stayed close behind, barking and biting at its tail.

Out on the paved road, a car stopped, and several tourists got out to watch this once in a lifetime scene! One man brought out a movie camera, and started filming the action. I have often wished that I had thought to get that man's contact information, because I would love to have a copy of that film. But at the time I was much more concerned about the safety of my little friend Swampy.

We were witnessing something that was just not meant to happen. Here was a small domestic dog actually chasing a huge alligator back into the swamp! I felt so proud of Swampy! The action continued over and over again for about one hundred yards with Swampy barking and biting at the gator's tail. The gator turned around as if to ward Swampy off, then swam again towards the swamp. It had become obvious that the gator wanted nothing to do with Swampy. All the poor thing wanted to do was go home.

When it was all over and the tourists had packed up their gear and left, Swampy came running back to me! I was so relieved that it was over, and I told Swampy,

"I am sure proud of you dog! Not many dogs could stand off a ten foot alligator like you did"

It has always amazed me that the alligator did not drown Swampy, and gobble him up. And usually, when a gator is after something, it will run at it, instead of half-way lunging like that gator did. And it is understandable that a dog will do its best to protect its territory from an invader. Maybe the gator simply was not hungry. Maybe it had seen enough of my home, or possibly it just realized that it was in the wrong place and did not need to be there. Whatever the reason, the ordeal was over. Swampy was safe.

I went back to the freezer, grabbed the gallon jug of ice and the crab bait, and put it in the cooler in the Jeep. We were ready to roll! As usual, Swampy sat shot gun. I praised Swampy over and over again. He snuggled up to me all the way to Clam Creek! We had both earned a few more swampwise points, and it was a good day for us on Jeykl Island![4]

Notes:

[1] I made my own ice by freezing gallon jugs full of water. This not only served to keep things cool, but as the ice would melt, it would also become the most welcome drinking water on those hot summer days.

[2] I knew this particular alligator. I had named it Jonas. Like Oscar it was a year 'round resident at the park. Neither one of them were captive. They were free to come and go as they pleased. Like many of the other wild 'gators', they chose to 'hang out' in the neighborhood, because they liked it there... more about those two later.

[3] Alligators have been known to travel at great speed for short distances. They can out run most breeds of dogs. Several times, at the park, when visitors had tied their pet dog outside the car, while they went on into the park, a gator made a meal out of the poor thing...lease, collar, and all!

[4] Had I known what the future held in store for Swampy, because of his attitude toward alligators, instead of praising him for what he had shown me, I would have most certainly sternly chastised him!

Part 4: Moments to Remember

Scattered throughout Florida, and Georgia there were dozens of serious, and sometimes "Stomp Down" hunting spots for collecting snakes. When I hunted them by myself, I couldn't cover all of them in one day. I'd leave the swamp before daylight, and often not make it home 'til the wee hours of the next morning.[1]

I was collecting snakes and selling the venomous ones to various venom extracting laboratories across the country, and the nonvenomous snakes to pet stores. There was not much money involved in it, but as the saying goes, "Every little bit helps." It was my hope, that although some of the snakes might die in captivity, some might live, and give a kid the incentive to learn more about snakes. It might serve to keep his interest up, and in later years he may find helpful ways to maintain their populations, in this ever expanding nation! In my book "Snake Hunter Snake Talk" I go into detail about that subject.

On many of those trips I did not take Swampy with me. There were too many things I did not want him to get into. Some of the spots were old abandoned farms, and there were a lot of chemicals, poisons, and who knows what lying around. Most of the old shacks were once the home of someone, and there were dirty clothes, dishes and trash scattered everywhere. It was really not a very healthy environment for me either. But besides all that, I was moving fast from spot to spot, with little time to spare. Swampy did not seem to mind staying home. He knew when I was going on a hunt out in the woods, away from all the trash, I would always take him with me.

I remember the long trips home, being alone and feeling worn out from all the walking and lifting, I had done. Many a time just to keep my spirits up I would think about the welcome I would receive when I got home. I really looked forward to those truly heart-warming, home coming moments. It will always be one of the fondest memories that Swampy ever gave to me.

From the main highway the last half mile of road to my house was as straight as an arrow. In the bright shining headlights of my jeep, I would see Swampy, a half a mile ahead, out in the middle of the road in front of our house, happily jumping up and down! And he'd be wagging that tail a mile a minute! He was always so overjoyed to see me. I felt the same way about my swampwise little friend!

When I reached my short driveway, I would allow him to jump in the jeep with me. He'd then proceed to warm my heart with another welcome home treat! He would talk to me. Oh how he would talk to me! It was as if he were telling me all that had happened while I was gone.

Skeeter the cat was always there to meet me too. She would not come out on the road to greet me, but she'd be at the front door, and as I opened it she would dart between my feet, and run into the house. Then, as Swampy jumped up in the kitchen chair jabbering as fast as he could, she would chime in with her harsh sounding meow for a while, too.

There were certain commands that Swampy needed to learn to obey. He knew early on what "No!" meant, and he would immediately stop whatever it was that he was doing. Because of the nature of my work, that was the most important command he needed to understand, especially when we were out in the woods hunting snakes, or handling venomous snakes at the house.

Another command he understood was "Heel!" As we walked from stump hole to stump hole, it was necessary for him to stay by my side, or slightly behind me. I could not let him get ahead of me for two reasons. One he might get bitten by a snake, and I sure did not want that to happen. And two, if there was a snake there he might scare it away before I arrived to catch it. We didn't want that to happen either. So he "heeled" really well!

He knew "Back seat!", "Get in the jeep!", "Sit!", "Stay!", "Down!", and "Go home!" We saw no need for the silly commands like "Roll over", "Sit", or "Shake!" He was a fine friend, and partner! And just like me he was surely becoming "Swampwise"!

I fed him two scoops of dry dog food each evening, while I made my supper. He would eagerly gobble down his meal, and quietly retreat to his corner, and lie down. He never begged for food. But of course he and Skeeter both always got some of the leftovers from supper. He didn't need to beg.

After supper, he and Skeeter were in the habit of going outside for leftovers. About the only other time either of them were in the house was when I first arrived home from work or from a trip.

One of my favorite habits was to sit on the steps to my front porch, and quietly think about the animals under my care at the park. I was constantly learning so much from them, and I spent a lot of time going over what I was learning. I would try to figure out why they did some of the things I'd see them do. Many times when Swampy would see me sitting there, he would quietly disappear into the woods. He'd make sure he was out of sight of me. Then he'd make a wide circle out there, and come back towards me from a different direction. As he came out of the woods he would crawl inch by inch on his belly quietly sneaking up on me. I think he knew that I knew he was doing that, but we both enjoyed the game anyway.

I'd make believe I didn't see him until he was right next to me. Then I would jump up hollering in make believe fright! It was just a rather senseless, but fun, game, and he loved it! I did too! He was a happy dog, and I was a happy man!

When I'd go to Clam Creek on Jeykl Island to catch food I would always take him with me. We could park the jeep right next to the water's edge. He'd spend most of the day under it, and out of the hot sun. He would watch me like a hawk.

Very few local people or island visitors ever went where I went on the island. There were rattlesnakes, cottonmouths, alligators, poison ivy and briars, and in the water sometimes sharks to contend with, and most people, especially vacationers don't care for those things. And that was just fine with me. I enjoyed my privacy immensly!

Every now and then, while I was out in the creek netting big blue claw crabs, digging clams, or casting for shrimp or fish, I'd hear him bark! I'd look up, and rarely, but sometimes it would be someone passing by. If they stopped or got too close to the crab basket, which I kept in the shade by the jeep, I would hear Swampy growl viciously at them, and they would leave. I did not encourage him to do that, but I did not discourage him either. He was protecting what was ours, and that is important!

Note:

[1] "Serious" meant a really good spot! "Stomp down" meant unbelievably good hunting spot! That's our snake hunter lingo! See my book "Snake Hunter Snake Talk".

Part 5: Swampy Is Shot By A Poacher

One night, after supper, I walked out on the porch thinking I'd play with Swampy for a little while. We had no porch lights, but in the dim glow from the lights inside the house I could see there was something different about the way Swampy looked. He seemed to be trembling, and he was panting rapidly! I hurried down the porch steps to him! With both hands I grabbed him by his shoulders as I always did. I felt something warm and sticky on both sides of his body, and I immediately came to the realization that he was bleeding! The blood was flowing from both sides of his body! I just about screamed,

"My, *God*! Swampy! You've been shot!"

I picked him up, and he winced in pain. As gently as I could I put him on the front seat of the jeep! I left everything at the house just as it was, including my wallet, and broke every speed limit getting up town to the vet's house! Along the way Swampy didn't whine much, but I knew he must have been in terrible pain.

We got to the veterinarian's house, and thank *God* the vet was home! We took Swampy inside, and placed him on the table. With some alcohol and tissues the vet wiped the blood away from his fur and his wounds, and examined him closely. In a moment that seemed an eternity, he turned to me and with a serious look on his face, he said,

"This dog has been shot with a high powered rifle! The bullet went right through his chest! You can thank your lucky stars that it did not hit any vital organs. He'll be in pain for a while, but he'll live!"

What a relief it was to know that Swampy would make it! The Vet gave him an injection of powerful pain medicine mixed with antibiotics. He gave me a handful of pills, a small bottle of iodine, and some cotton swabs, to use over the next few days. He said no bandage was required.

All the way home I kept my hand on Swampy's head, and saying many a prayer of thanks to *God* that he'd live!

There is a reason for everything! And I was sure I knew the reason for what had just happened to my best friend Swampy.

Several nights before I had been awakened by Swampy's people bark and the honking of a horn as a pickup truck pulled up into my yard! It was about midnight, and at my door was one of the park's summer part time employees. He was a young man of sixteen, and he was badly shaken, and out of breath! In a frightened voice he tried to explain what had just happened!

He said that he, and his step brother had been out fire hunting in the swamp, and that they had killed seventeen deer. They were gathering them up one by one, and throwing them into the truck bed. Suddenly bright lights came on all around them, and a voice over a loud speaker told them to lay their weapons down, and stand still with their hands over their heads! They had been caught red handed!

He stood there as instructed, but his step brother, who by the way was an ex- Marine, ran off into the swamp and disappeared! The game warden checked his ID, and since he was a miner, and they knew who he was, and where he lived, he was told to take the truck and drive home immediately! He stopped by my place on his way to tell me what had happened, and that I should expect his step brother to be there at my house at any moment, needing a ride home!

I cussed him out for involving me in that mess, but I promised that if his step brother did arrive at my place, I'd give him a ride home to Waycross.

About three o'clock a.m. Swampy's people bark awakened me again, and the culprit was at my door! He was soaking wet with sweat, had cuts and bruises on his face, and his clothes were torn. He had just crawled and run through almost ten miles of Okefenokee Swamp! I told him to get in the jeep. Swampy and I jumped in with him, and I drove him into town as I had promised I would do.

On the way he asked me over and over again to promise not to tell anyone that I had seen him. And I told him over and over again that I would keep his secret, unless it would get me in trouble along with him.

After dropping him off at his house, I drove back toward home. Along the way I was thinking to myself,

"Seventeen deer! That's a lot of deer meat! They must have been selling it!"

After thinking it over, I wasn't sure I wanted to keep their secret! What they had done was not right! It wasn't fair to the animals, and it wasn't fair to the rest of the law abiding licensed Georgia hunters! As I debated this with myself, I was suddenly interrupted, and what I saw up ahead made my mind up for me!

At the junction of the highway, and my swamp road, I could see flashing blue lights! It was a road block! I knew immediately what it meant!

They pulled me over, and I was asked if I had just carried someone home! I knew that if I gave them the wrong answer, sooner or later I would hang from the same tree as the others. I sure didn't want that, so I told the game warden the truth.

I was then asked if I would testify to that in court. I told them that yes I would testify, but only if it became absolutely necessary for me to do so.

They picked up my friend's step brother the next morning. They confiscated his truck, his driver's license, and his rifle. His court date was set for the following month, and he was out on bail that afternoon! Swampy was shot a few nights later!

After I brought Swampy home from the vet's house, I laid him on my bed, and made him as comfortable as I could. Then I went to the closet and pulled out my forty-five automatic pistol and a box of bullets. I spent the next hour cleaning the weapon, and loading several clips of ammo. I placed a live round in the chamber, shoved a full clip in the handle, put the gun on safety, and placed it under my pillow next to Swampy. Then I lay back down to take advantage of the few remaining hours until day light to get some sleep.

But I couldn't sleep. I was too uptight about what had just happened. The reason I had loaded my gun was simply to protect myself. I was angry, but I knew that if I was fool enough to take revenge myself, it would only serve to get me in trouble with the law, and I did not want that. If the man was convicted over the killing of all those poor deer, it would be payback enough for me. I spent the rest of that night restlessly considering my options.

The next morning I was given permission from the park to go up town to the court house, and apply for a concealed weapons permit. I was happily surprised when I was told by the sheriff that in Georgia I was not required to have a permit to carry a loaded gun. So I did not have to wait to be legal. I already was legal! Over the next few years I kept that weapon with me at all times.

The man had his day in court. As it turned out the law did not need my testimony, and I did not attend the trial. He was found guilty, and fined $2,500, and sentenced to three months in jail. His much younger step brother was given a year's probation.

A week or so after the sentence had been imposed, the younger one came by my house to warn me that his step brother had told him that "I'd better make my peace with the Lord, because when he gets out he's going to come after me!"

Needless to say that information really upset me! I didn't know whether to be frightened or angry about the situation. I was living a good, honest, happy, healthy, and exciting life. I did not need the aggravation of waiting for someone to "come get me!" I decided to settle this "Come and get me" stuff right away! I went straight to the jailhouse, and asked to see him!

The officer in charge told me that visiting hours were over, but he'd go get him anyhow. He was brought into the room glaring at me! I glared right back at him, and I immediately said to him,

"You shot my dog! Didn't you? And what's this about you coming to get me?"

It took a moment, but he retorted,

"Yeah! You better make your peace because when I get out of here the first thing I'm going to do is come after you!"

I try to be fair-minded, and keep an even keel. Violence has always been my last resort, but I could not help myself in this situation, and I just about screamed at him,

"I ain't going to wait 'til then! How about right now?"

And I jumped at him! He really surprised me, because instead of grappling with me, he turned and ran away from me! The officer in charge rushed in! He got between us, and said words to the effect, "You can't do that here!" He took his prisoner back to his cell, and told me to please leave!

Months later I heard a rumor that the sheriff of Ware County Georgia was complaining about Okefenokee Joe coming to his jail threatening, and upsetting his prisoners!

For a long time after that incident I stayed as alert as I possibly could. I kept my side arm with me at all times. From the way he acted in the jail house, I halfway figured he would not come after me head on! It would more likely be an ambush, or with a gang, or some other cowardly way. At this writing, over forty years have gone by since that incident. I have not seen nor heard from him since, but I'm still ready for him!

Thank God, Swampy healed, and lived on!

Part 6: Swampy the Survivor

The old familiar saying that "Cats have nine lives" could also apply to dogs. In the short time Swampy was with me he survived many a close brush with danger, and near death.

He'd confronted a huge alligator, he'd been shot, and he'd been bitten by a very deadly cottonmouth! He was swampwise and a tough little guy. He had survived those incidents and more! He had become truly swampwise!

Like most dogs, Swampy loved to chase and snap at flying insects. On our front porch in the swamp, especially in late spring, he had a field day every day. There were hundreds of biting yellow flies for him to chase. It was always fun to watch him do it. He'd miss most of them, but sometimes he'd catch one! If he happened to catch one, he would usually end up swallowing it.

One day I was sitting on the steps of our front porch talking to him about life in general. I was hugging him, and he was listening to me counting our blessings. I said,

"You know, Swampy, our life is wonderful here in the Okefenokee. We've got love, a roof over our heads, and plenty of food. We're free to come and go as we please. There's an ocean an hour away, where we can go to catch sea food any time we want to. We can go snake hunting! Life is good here in the swamp! The only thing missing here is a good woman!"

And with a puzzled look Swampy would look at me as if to say, "What? Are you crazy?"

But it was true. I really did miss the love, and the comforting touch of a good woman. I wasn't lonely all the time, just some times.

We heard a buzzing sound much louder than a yellow fly would make, and Swampy went after it. I told him he'd better leave that one alone, it was a red wasp, and those things pack one heck of a wallop! They've put people in the hospital! One hit me in the forearm while I was in my garden, pulling my dried up snap bean vines down. I ended up in the emergency ward at the hospital!

Swampy, of course had no idea what I was saying, and unluckily he caught the wasp in his mouth! It immediately stung him on the tongue!

He gave a frightened yelp of pain, dropped the wasp, and began running around the yard yelping and whining his head off! Poor guy, he was in excruciating pain! His tongue and his lower jaw had swelled up beyond belief! I felt so sorry for him. I didn't have any dog pain pills, or anything in the house to put on his tongue to relieve the pain. I tried to get him to let me put some cool mud on it, but he kept shaking his head, and spitting it out!

I remembered that I had some oxycodone left over from the

time my lawnmower sent a huge rusty nail deep into the calf of my right leg! I ran to our medicine cabinet, and found the bottle! Opening it as I ran back outside, I took out a pill, and broke it in half! I grabbed Swampy, forced his mouth open, and shoved the half pill in! I held his swollen mouth shut and stroked his throat until I knew he had swallowed it.

It took about a half an hour for his pain to subside. I'm not a doctor, and I had no idea what effect the pill would have on him. All I knew was that my dog was in pain, and I had to do something about it. So I did!

Thank God! With no noticeable ill effect on Swampy it worked! I remember thinking,

"I'll bet he learned his lesson. He'll never go after a red wasp again. He's too swampwise to do that!" But I was wrong! He was frequently out there in the yard, howling in pain from the sting of things he never did learn to leave alone!

In the day time there was a lot of traffic on the paved road out in front of our house. Swampy never chased cars, and most of the time he stayed off the paved road. That's why I was so surprised one day when I came home at lunch time to pick up a few things, and found Swampy lying on the porch breathing hard and whining! As I knelt down beside him, I saw that some of the fur on the right side of his head was missing, and he was bleeding slightly. When I touched his shoulder, he yelped in pain! I said,

"Hey, little guy! Did you get hit by a car or something?"

Fearing his shoulder might be broken, and that he might have concussion, I picked him up carefully, and put him in the jeep. I drove to the veterinarian's office, and had him checked out.

He had no concussion, just a severe bump on his head. His shoulder was sprained, and required a splint. The vet patched him up, gave me some pain pills and antibiotics as usual, and advised me to keep him quiet for a few days, and he'd be alright. Once again Swampy had survived!

Okefenokee Joe

Part 7: Be a Long Time Forgettin'

One evening, as usual, I walked out on the front porch, and called to swampy. I had a few leftovers from supper for him. Skeeter had already had her share. Swampy didn't come to me. I remember thinking "He wanted "out" right after he ate his supper. He's probably doing his business, he'll be along shortly."

But he didn't come home. After a while I went outside to look for him. But he was nowhere around. Skeeter was there, rubbing on my knee, and purring, but no Swampy.

Everything else was around. I could hear a barred owl in the distance. That same owl had been around the place ever since I moved in. I knew him by the song I'd hear him sing. It wasn't quite right, or all together for a barred owl song. Always a note or two would be missing. I guess for some reason he never learned how to do it right like a barred owl should. I called him "the demented owl". It was fun to listen to him, and I was glad he was around. I was wishing Swampy was. Where was he?

"Swaaaaampy!"

I would yell, at the top of my lungs. But, no answer. I walked all around the area calling for him to no avail. It was now past our bedtime, and I had to work the next day, so I was forced to turn in. I didn't sleep much though. I was worried about my little Swampy. I got up several times throughout the night calling for him. But still no answer!

The next morning I was up early. Skeeter was on the porch in the dog house, but no Swampy. I drove the dirt roads looking for him, and calling his name, until it was time to go to work.

Swampy was on my mind all that day. I kept promising myself that when I got home he'd be wagging his tail, and jumping down from the porch to say 'hello' to me. And at quitting time I hurried home to be with him!

But he wasn't there. That's when a serious feeling of complete hopelessness and helplessness really started to sink in. I was realizing that I had lost him. But where could he be?

Could a tourist have picked him up, and taken him home?

Could he be in a fur trapper's steel trap somewhere? Where could he be? Could a gator have caught him?

Then, in horror, I remembered the day Swampy chased Jonas up the canal, and back into the swamp. I remember thinking back then that Swampy might have learned the wrong lesson about his relationship with an alligator. He might think he could chase any gator, and get away with it. "Oh, Lord", I thought!. "Please don't let that be what happened!"

Two full anxious, heartbreaking days and nights went by. Still, no swampy. I had spent hours and hours searching high and low for him. I thought he was lost from me forever. But, finally I found him.

Driving along, not far from the house, I spotted several black vultures circling over a small pond. I stopped the jeep, got out, and walked over to the pond to get a closer look. My heart skipped a beat when I saw something brown floating in the black water. Nearby I could see the two eyes of a gator. Its whole body was under water. Only its eyes were visible. It seemed to be guarding that brown thing floating in the water out there.

I drove home, and quickly hooked up my boat trailer to the jeep. I kept a twelve foot 'john' boat in it for fishing trips. Just as fast as I could I drove back to the scene. I put the boat in the water, and paddled over towards that brown thing. The gator that was guarding it disappeared under the water, and swam away. It wanted no trouble with me.

As I paddled closer to that floating object, I began to smell the terrible sickening odor of a dead animal. It was all but burning my up my nostrils as I picked that floating brown thing up out of the water.

It was Swampy alright! Or better said, what was left of him! He fell apart in my hands. Oh I was in total despair. I was a mental wreck.

I tearfully put him in the boat with me, and paddled back to shore. The gator was still hiding somewhere. At least I couldn't see it.

I buried Swampy in our front yard in a place of honor, under the big live oak tree. His memory will live forever in my heart.

Part 8: Swampy's Epilogue

Every now and then, even after all these years, I'll take a little time off, and go to the Okefenokee, and visit a place I call 'Swampy Lake". And I'll look out there in the water at that alligator that took my dog Swampy so many years ago, and I will remember.

Yes! That's right! That gator is still out there! And if you are wondering why, I will tell you why, right now!

If that gator had crawled up into my yard after Swampy, I would have shot him on the spot. We've got the right to defend what is ours. And we should! But that is not how it happened!

That alligator was out there in its chosen spot, in the wilds of the Okefenokee, and minding its own business. It was working at its job, doing what *God* had created it to do. It's a predator! And as such, one of its duties is to help control the population of animals in its territory. What happened to Swampy was not the alligator's fault!

It was Swampy! One second my best friend forgot to be Swampwise! He forgot to look out!

The same thing could happen to anybody! Even someone as old as me! If I forget for just one second, to look up and down the street, before I begin to cross it, everyone knows what would happen if a truck were to come by at that very moment!

Are we going to spend the rest of our life hating all the trucks we see? Are we going to go out tonight, and do some "truck huntin'"? Are we going to get some revenge by shooting a few trucks?

I don't hate that alligator, but I am sure sorry it happened!
Here's to you, Swampy!

CHAPTER 3
SKEETER THE CAT

Part 1: Finding Skeeter

One morning, on my day off, the park manager stopped by, and asked me to come out to the park, and help clean up a mess some of our visitors had left in the picnic area. I dropped what I was doing, told Swampy to "Get in the jeep", and drove on out to the park. I took him just about everywhere I went. He was good company, well behaved, and seldom any trouble for me. So he went with me to the picnic area that morning, and I am sure glad he did!

While I was helping to pick up the litter, I heard Swampy start scratching at something, and whining. Looking up I saw him deeply engrossed in sniffing, and pawing at an empty fifty-five gallon trash drum next to the water fountain. I walked over to see what was so intensely attracting him, and there in the bottom of that empty trash drum, along with several thousand mosquitoes, was a tiny, lost and forlorn looking calico kitten!

I picked her up out of that dirty drum. She was no bigger than a Coco Cola can, and covered with those pesky little insects. She was so tiny that she actually fit right in the palm of my upturned hand! I held her up eye level with me, and as I brushed the mosquitoes off of her, I said,

"You're a cute little rascal! You're gonna' come home with us, and be part of our family. Your job will be catching mice and rats, and since I found you covered with mosquitoes your name is going to be "Skeeter!"

We took her home, and she became 'boss' the minute we got there!

She was a beautiful many colored, four week old calico kitten. But she was filthy, and covered with mosquito and tick bites. The first thing I did when got her home was to give her a bath in ivory soap! And thinking she might be hungry, I put a bowl of fresh milk in front of her. To my surprise, as hungry as she was, she turned her nose up at it, and walked away.

Not knowing what else to do, I took her by the nap of the neck, and placed her nose closer to the milk. But she struggled with me, so I turned her loose. She immediately turned her back on it, and walked away again. She just wasn't interested in milk.

I left the bowl on the floor in the kitchen, hoping that maybe she would come back to it later, and drink it.

There was quite a bit of time left before supper, so I went out back where I kept all my camping, and snake hunting gear. That's where I was earlier that day when I was called out to the park.

With proper care most of my equipment would last a long time. I brought out my 10' x 12' canvas tent, and spread it out on the ground in the afternoon sun. Swampy and I had just gotten back home that morning. We had been down in South Florida hunting snakes. It was raining when we broke camp, so I had temporarily rolled the wet tent up and brought it home. It needed to dry out completely before I stored it away until our next trip. Otherwise mold would develop on it, and ruin it.[1]

I could hear little Skeeter in the house meowing constantly. Unlike most kittens her meow was loud, and the demanding tone of it sounded to me as if she thought she was in charge of things around the house. I wasn't sure if I liked that or not. But I was not going to let it worry me.

When suppertime rolled around, I went back inside to get things ready for our evening meal. Skeeter was still meowing, and pacing around in the living room. I noticed she had still not touched the milk I had left out for her. It had long since begun to curdle, and it smelled a little rancid, so I took it outside and dumped it. Then I poured out some more milk in a different bowl, and placed it on the floor, hoping Skeeter would find it, and drink it. I was thinking to myself, "She's got to be hungry, why doesn't she eat?"

I was living by myself those days, and to make life easier many a time I would cook up enough chicken or beef stew to last several days. That made our suppers much easier to prepare. My stew had all the necessary daily nutrients in it, and it surely made life easier for me. Several nights each week all I needed to do for supper was to heat up the stew. This of course, was after I had been given a refrigerator by the kind folks at the Baptist Church in Waycross.

Tonight's meal was chicken stew. And like most day or two old stews, it was more delicious than the first serving!

I was noticing that my little kitten's bowl was still full of milk. It was obvious to me by now, that she just did not want milk. I could not imagine why she didn't. Cats are supposed to love milk, aren't they? What happened next was an amazing, enlightening, and problem- solving surprise for me! A piece of chicken slipped off of my fork, and before I could catch it it fell to the floor. Quick as a wink, before Swampy could grab it, little Skeeter had it in her jaws. She ran over to a corner, and feverishly began devouring it! Inadvertently I had learned the answer to my dilemma over what to feed her. And it suddenly dawned on me that the irritating and demanding meow we were hearing must have meant she wanted meat not milk!

It goes against all the rules of kitten-raising I had ever heard. She could not have been more than four weeks old, and she was refusing milk, and eating solid foods! And she was also meowing!

Well, now we knew what to feed her. The next day I hurried into town, and picked up a dozen cans of cat food.

For almost three wonderful, adventurous, and happy years, I

would sing, "Okefenokee Georgia, population three: Swampy the dog, Skeeter the cat, and me."[2]

Note:

[1] Many times throughout the year we would go on snake hunts. My job at the park did not pay much, and the sale of snakes would bring in much needed extra income.

[2] Excerpt from Joe's recording of "Swampy the dog, Skeeter the cat, and me".

Part 2: Skeeter and the Opossum

One chilly winter evening I laid my blanket down in front of the fireplace, preparing for a good night's sleep. It was dark outside and I had a nice warm fire going. Swampy and Skeeter were already asleep in their wooden dog house on the front porch. At least I thought they were. I felt relaxed and comfortable, and life was good!

Suddenly I was disturbed by a loud racket coming from out in the chicken house! My chickens were awake and upset about something, and there was quite a commotion going on! Swampy, no longer asleep, was barking his "critter bark"! I was pretty sure what it was that had them so riled up!

Several nights before, I had seen a huge boar opossum out there, snooping around their fenced in pen. I had shooed him off with a shotgun blast over his head. My guess was that he must have finally found a way to get inside the pen with my chickens! That would never do!

It was my habit to sleep in just my undershorts and a t-shirt. Chilly outside or not, I didn't have time to get dressed! I quickly slipped into my tennis shoes, put my head lamp on, grabbed my loaded twelve gauge shotgun off the wall mount, and ran out back to the chicken house! Things had quieted down some, but I could tell by the sounds they were making, that the chickens were still upset.

I opened the screen door to the chicken pen, and stepped in. Out of habit, I closed the door behind me. The first thing I saw really took me by surprise! I was shocked! Mainly because it simply didn't make sense!

It was the opossum all right! He had dug his way under the one inch chicken wire fence. That in itself was a real surprise for me, because when I reconstructed my chicken pen, I had purposely buried the wire over a foot under the ground all around it. I thought nothing would bother to dig that deep to get at my chickens. I thought wrong, because here was a huge opossum in the pen with my chickens! But that is not all that surprised me!

The opossum was lying motionless on the ground! To my dismay, lying beside it was one of my best Rhode Island Red laying hens still writhing in death throes! Her name was "Betty". Obviously something must have seriously frightened the opossum, because it was lying there "playing possum"!

I had dealt with those animals before. As a matter of fact at that time, I was caring for two male opossums out at the park. I called them Pete, and Repeat, and they had taught me a lot about opossums. One important thing I learned early on, is that they can give a serious bite when inclined to do so. I know that because I'd been 'possum bit' on several occasions.

In the wild, unlike most furry creatures, they seldom stalk their prey, and even more seldom do they make a kill. Unless its prey is weak, or defenseless, like a chicken! Their diet consists mostly of animals that have already died from other sources. Most wild opossums reek with the foul odor of carrion. Opossums don't care if the nose of a carnivore finds them or not. They are safe from most predators, because almost nothing in the woods will eat 'possum meat'.

The hairless tail of an opossum is remarkably strong. It will often sleep upside down the entire night on the branch of a tree, hanging by it's tail. In recent years it was discovered that the opossum's habit of "playing dead" is not a conscious effort. It seems the opossum cannot help passing out when it is terribly frightened. Its nervous system shuts down automatically.

So this opossum lying seemingly unconscious, on the ground in my chicken pen was not just "playing possum." Something had really frightened it!

Its harsh meow led me straight to the guilty party! At least I assumed she was the guilty party. She had been quiet up until now. She must have come into the pen through the same hole that the opossum had done! I couldn't help but wonder how in the world my tiny calico cat could have frightened that big opossum. To this day I still marvel about that.

I grabbed the opossum by the tail, and as I opened the door to leave, Skeeter ran under my feet, and out of the pen. I put the opossum in an empty fifty five gallon drum, and screwed the lid on tightly. The drum had plenty of air holes in it because I had used it many times to transport other small animals.

The next day I drove south of Race Pond, and turned the now wide awake opossum loose on the edge of the swamp.

I'll always wonder if it was Skeeter that had put that huge opossum to sleep, and if it was her, how in the world did she do it?

Part 3: Who's Afraid of the Lightning?

From the very beginning, when we first brought Skeeter home with us, Swampy had taken a 'big brother' protective attitude towards her. As time went on it became obvious that the two of them had developed a strong, loving bond. That is quite different from most dog and cat stories. But we were living a different lifestyle than most people who own dogs and cats.

Many a morning I'd wake up, and look out my front door, and on my front porch I would see happiness and contentment at its finest. Swampy and Skeeter would be cuddled up together, and sound asleep in the little wooden house I had built for Swampy. What a beautiful, heart-warming sight it was! Love can be wonderful! And to see it, and know it every day is even more wonderful!

For the most part the two of them lived outside, and they seemed to enjoy it. At feeding time, and several other special occasions, they would come inside with me. One such extra special occasion occurred on a hot and sultry mid-August afternoon.

I was sitting on the steps of the front porch, enjoying the scenery, and watching Swampy and Skeeter at play over by the wood pile. They sure knew how to have a good time, and it was real a pleasure to watch them. Skeeter would slap Swampy's tail, and he'd turn around, and chase her a little ways. Sometimes they played with an old sock like two dogs would do. They were fun, and I enjoyed them.

Looking up at the huge Live Oak tree that shaded our house, I noticed its leaves had begun turning slightly upside down. That is a strong indication that rain might be coming. The green tree frogs began to sing, and the cricket frogs joined in. We could also hear the sound of a narrow mouth toad. Out in the Okefenokee the daytime singing of the frogs is another very accurate barometer. It usually means that rain is on its way, or, as in this case, was just about here!

Another indication that rain is on it's way, especially in the summertime is the distinct sudden change in the air around us. As it clouds up the air begins to take on that familiar damp, 'earthy' odor.

Sure enough, a moment later we heard the ominous crackling sound of thunder not far away. Clouds quickly began to form, blocking out the sun, and the wind suddenly picked up speed. We knew it was coming our way, and it was coming fast![1]

Skeeter was paying no attention to the weather. She was now over by the big live oak tree playing with an acorn that one of our squirrel neighbors had mistakenly left behind.

The first lightning bolt struck, just before the rain started pouring down. It was especially frightening because it struck just a short ways from where we were. Then the heavy down pour began.

Our front porch had a roof over it, and I found myself running towards it. Swampy was hot on my heels. Skeeter was still playing over by the oak tree.

The second lightning bolt struck! It felt like it had landed right on top of us! And it almost did! It actually hit the huge oak tree where Skeeter was playing, not ten feet away from us! It went clean through the tree, splitting a part of its trunk, and into the ground below.

For one horrible second I saw Skeeter crinch up, with every hair on her body standing straight out! In panic and pain she uttered a loud cry of helplessness, and collapsed in a heap on the ground! My poor little cat had been struck by lightning!

I jumped off the porch, and ran over to her. She was lying there on the ground motionless. As I picked her up I could not tell if she was breathing! Hurrying into the house with her in my arms, close to my heart, I was praying,

"Oh, *God* ! Oh, *God*, please don't let her die"!

Once inside the house, I laid her limp body gently down on the couch, and rushed to the closet to get her a towel! As I was drying her off, thank *God* she began to breathe! She was unconscious, yet every now and then her body would move in a jerking fashion. I was not sure what else I could do for her. But since she was sound asleep, I decided to just let her rest there on the couch.

Every now and then I would check on her, especially to see if she was still breathing. In my desperately worried mind I did not know if she would live or not. She stayed unconscious on the couch for two days. Not sure that she would make it, I worried about her, and prayed for her the whole time.

While I sat there watching her, I began remembering endearing things about my little cat Skeeter. like the night I was sitting at the kitchen table just after supper, and I picked her up, and put her on my lap, and began to pet her. She jumped off my lap, and I called out to her,

"Swampwise"

"Skeeter come back here!"

But as cats will sometimes do, she just ignored me. I called to her four or five times, and I was remembering now how angry I became, and thoughtlessly hollered at her, "You remind me of my ex-wife! She acted the same way!"

And I took off one of my boots, and threw it at her! *Thank God* it did not hit her, but it did hit the picture of my Mom & Dad that hung on the wall just above where she was sitting. I was so proud of that picture, and now it needed a new glass, and maybe a new frame! I was sorry for doing it, and I apologized to Skeeter for getting angry with her, and scaring her like that.

I remembered the time she brought a mouse into the house, and laid it at my feet. It seemed as though she was giving it to me. And I thought maybe I should give her something in return. So I got a half full can of cat food out of the refrigerator, put it in her bowl, and gave it to her. She didn't hesitate. She ate that cold canned cat food in a hurry! A few days later she came in the house with another mouse, and laid it on the floor in front of me! I did not want it to become a habit, so I ignored her gift. She did it one more time, and I ignored her again.

When Swampy and I would take short walks, she would sometimes trail along. At times she even got ahead of us. And I remembered the several times that I told Swampy to heel, and Skeeter slapped his tail. I was remembering all the things that made her so precious to me. And as I sat there it almost made me cry, when I thought of the time that Skeeter actually talked to me. It was one evening just after supper, when she walked into the kitchen, and instead of just meowing like she usually did, she plain as day said,

"I wanna' go out now!"

I was shocked! I could not believe what I was hearing. So I asked her, "What?"

And she said again, plain as day, "I wanna' go out now!"

And I asked, "You want to go out now?"

And believe it or not she said, "Yes! I wanna' go out now!"

You can bet I immediately "Let her out now!"

Thank God, she finally woke up! And when she did, she climbed down off the couch. And once again we were hearing that familiar Skeeter the Cat demanding meow! I picked her up, and held her in my arms, she began to purr contentedly. She seemed to have no ill after effects from her near death experience with lightning. And apparently she had already forgotten about it.

The whole time she had been unconscious she had been without water or food, so I brought her food and water bowls in from the porch, and filled them up. Purring like a happy healthy cat, she ate and drank voraciously. I felt greatly relieved. *Thank God* Skeeter was back to normal.[2]

Shortly after that lightning incident Swampy would be gone!

Notes:

[1] On a hot afternoon in the swamp, especially in mid-summer, heavy thunder storms are not unlikely. Hail usually came with it. We'd sometimes see hail stones the size of a golf ball!

[2] Not many humans struck by lightning will live to tell about it. Here was a tiny calico cat that survived a direct hit, and in two days she was back to normal again!

Part 4: Cats Teach Lessons, Too!

One afternoon Swampy and I were returning from a snake hunt with empty snake boxes. We had not even seen a snake all that day. Yet as I pulled into my driveway I could hear the distinct shrill buzzing sound of a deadly rattlesnake's rattles. Swampy heard it, too, and he began to bark.

I had no snakes with me, so I knew it was a wild one somewhere in my front yard! It was hard to tell exactly where the sound was coming from, so to hear more clearly I told Swampy to stop barking, and I turned off the engine.

Looking in the direction that the sound was coming from, I immediately located the snake. It was not far from the steps of my front porch. It was a rattler alright. It was an eastern diamondback, and a big one. It was coiled up, and rattling in the ready position. But I was in for another surprise because that's not all I saw.

My tiny calico cat Skeeter was walking around that huge rattlesnake in a complete circle. The sight of her that close to a deadly snake, and a big one at that, caused me to fear for her life. I had never seen her do something like that before! I thought to myself that I had better get her away from that monster. But she seemed to know exactly what she was doing. She was staying just out of reach of its striking distance.[1]

The snake was highly alert, and in a magnificent, defensive stance. It was coiled tightly, with its head and part of its body up about ten inches off the ground. Its tail was vibrating rapidly, and it was watching Skeeter's every move. But I noticed right away that it was not attacking her!

I decided to allow this scenario play out without any interference from me. I was really fond of Skeeter, and I certainly did not want anything to happen to her. But I wanted to learn the truth about the actual behavior of a rattlesnake in a situation like this one was in.

Praying for Skeeter's safety, I sat in my jeep not more than twenty feet away, and watched. Swampy stayed in the jeep with me. He, too, was watching silently.

Skeeter paid no attention to me. The snake didn't either. They both acted as if they didn't even know I was there. My little calico cat kept walking around that snake. The snake, obviously attempting to protect itself, would turn completely around in its coils to watch her every move. But never once did it attempt to harm her.

I noticed that each time Skeeter would move at a slower pace, the snake would begin to slow the intensity of its rattling. If she stopped and stood still, the snake would eventually stop rattling. When she would start to move again, the snake would immediately begin to shake its tail. There was nothing blocking the way between that snake and Skeeter. That rattlesnake could have crawled over and bitten Skeeter in a heartbeat! But it didn't do that. This is where I began to understand that it is fear, and not anger, that will cause a rattlesnake vibrate its tail.[2]

After about twenty minutes of this scenario, I finally thought I had seen enough, and I decided it was time that I should do something about it. Just at that moment little Skeeter the Cat herself decided to do something about it.

My tiny calico cat calmly turned her back on that huge and deadly rattlesnake, and ever so slowly she began to walk away. The snake did not follow her. It didn't move from its spot. It remained there rattling, in that same defensive coil. The further away she went, the more passive the snake's rattling became. This made it even more convincing to me that the snake had been vibrating its tail in fear. It was quite obvious by now that it simply wanted nothing whatsoever to do with Skeeter the cat!

Just before Skeeter disappeared into the bushes, she turned around and she looked straight into my eyes! It was as if she had finished teaching me what I needed to know about snakes! I never saw her do that again!

What did she teach me?

For the first time in my life it was proven to me that a snake will not attack something too big to eat. The snake probably did not know what Skeeter was, but it certainly recognized that she was too big to eat! At the same time it was shown to me for the first time in my life that although the snake would not attack her, it would not run from her either.

Skeeter was truly swampwise! And after witnessing her enlightening encounter with that huge rattlesnake, I began to more deeply understand the actions, and the reactions of all the creatures under my care. I shall always be grateful to Skeeter for the great, and wonderful wildlife behavior lessons she taught me that day.

"Swampwise"

Notes:

[1] Most of our venomous snakes are capable of reaching about a third of the length of their body when they strike. On a smooth surface they might slide a little. If that happened, though, they probably would not hit what they are aiming at!

[2] See Fear versus anger in the chapter entitled Nature's Rules of Conduct.

Picture courtesy of Betty Frady
The Deadly and Fearsome Eastern Diamondback Rattlesnake

CHAPTER 4
PRINCESS SUWANEE

Part 1: Cryin' Wolf

I am a light sleeper. One night I was suddenly brought wide awake by the ominous sound of Swampy's suspicious growl. He had been out in the yard, but now he was up on the porch. I seldom ever heard him growl like that, so I knew immediately that something important was going on. I sat up in bed, and as I listened I began to hear another sound coming from way out there in the swamp! I realized then what was making my little swampwise friend so upset! Cold chills began running up and down my spine. A mournful, wailing, lone wolf like sound was penetrating the usual early spring sounds of the night! It was emanating from way out there in the foreboding darkness of the Okefenokee Swamp![1]

According to the Georgia State Game Commission the Red Wolf, which had once roamed across the entire Southeastern United States, had not been seen in or near the Okefenokee Swamp in many years. Like the Whooping Crane, and the Ivory Billed Woodpecker it had been brought to the brink of extinction by the greedy and foolish hand of civilized man. And for that reason what I was hearing most certainly could not have been a wolf! Or could it?

It was affecting Swampy, too, but in a different way. Though he was a domestic dog, he had begun trying to imitate that eerie sound. He was not very good at it, but he was trying. He reminded me of a young rooster learning how to crow for the first time. It'll make a lot of almost comical mistakes until it finally gets it right. But I did not want Swampy learning to howl correctly!

Suddenly it dawned on me that whatever that creature was, it was possibly calling to Swampy to come join it out there in the wilderness. Its plaintiff howl was sounding as if it was saying,

"Swampy! Come on out here with me! Learn to enjoy the good life! Come and be wild and free with me!" And I was definitely not having any of that!

I ran outside, grabbed Swampy by the collar, and as I brought him into the house with me I said,

"Swampy! You don't want to be a wolf! Do You?"

I could tell he was really being affected by that 'call of the wild' out there. It was as if some primeval instinct way down deep inside of him, had suddenly come alive. I was not going to let that happen. I loved that little short legged dog, and I was not going to lose him to some wild wolf like thing out there in the swamp!

Eventually the howling ceased, but I was determined to keep Swampy inside the house, until I knew for certain that whatever it was out there was gone. He woke me up several times during the rest of the night, scratching on the door, but I was not about to let him out.

The next day went by with nothing unusual happening. Using the park's phone, I called the State Game Commission, and the Georgia Forestry Service to see if anything new data had come in regarding the status of the Red Wolf. Both offices informed me that there was nothing new. And until I knew for certain what was making that haunting sound out there, I decided not to tell anyone about it.

Swampy spent the day with me in the Serpentarium at the park. I was not going to let him out of my sight. I took him for several walks, and during my lectures he stayed in my office with the door locked.

That evening, after supper, just before dark, I took him for a walk, using a leash to keep him by my side. That wild creature out there really had me concerned.

The whole time that swampy had been with me he had been an 'outdoors' dog. I would bring him in for supper, and for a little while when I came home from work or a trip. Other than that though, he had seldom been in the house. It was my belief that he would be much happier and healthier living out in the fresh air. Besides that, he was my 'first line of defense'. I depended on his bark to alert me of any approaching danger, especially at night. Tonight though, he would stay in the house with me.[2]

I always liked to sleep with my bedroom windows wide open.

Fresh air is healthy air. That night I was enjoying the usual late spring night sounds. I could hear the call of the chuck will's widow, the mixed choruses of the barking and green tree frogs, southern cricket and bronse frogs, and an occasional southern oak toad. All of these songs are sweet music to my ears. But that night I was also listening for something I did not want to hear.

Everything was right, until about three am, when the howling began again. This time it was a little closer. Swampy began to imitate the sound, and I did my best to quiet him down. He persisted and started scratching on the front door. He wanted out, but I was not about to do that. After about an hour the howling ceased, and all was quiet again, including Swampy.

An hour later the howling began again. This time it was even closer to our house. I jumped out of bed! I tied Swampy to the bed post, grabbed my 30 30 Winchester Rifle, and my headlamp, and rushed outside.[3]

The sound seemed to be coming from over behind the outhouse. It was that close! I shined my light over that way, and caught a brief glimpse of two green eyes, as the creature turned and ran off. Thinking maybe I could get a look its tracks, I hurried on over to where it had been. But in the darkness, even with my headlamp I could not find any tracks. I went back into the house, locked the door, untied Swampy, and went back to bed. There was no more howling for the rest of the night.

In the morning I walked to the outhouse, and looked for tracks. I found a few. It was a canine alright! But not knowing the difference between domestic dog and wolf tracks, the creature was still a mystery to me. Needless to say, Swampy spent the day with me out at the park again.

That night the howling began just after dark. I tied Swampy up, and ran outside with my headlamp, and my rifle! This time I spotted it, and got a brief but good look at it. To my surprise, and relief, It was not a wolf! It was a very lean female German shepherd dog that had apparently gone wild.

Thank God! What a blessing it was to know now, that the creature that had been haunting us those past few nights was not a wild wolf!

I went back into the house, and almost joyfully hung my rifle, and my headlamp back up on the rack above the fireplace! As I was untying Swampy, the thought occurred to me that maybe, because it seemed to be coming closer each night, that wild dog was trying to make friends with us. It was a domestic breed, and maybe it was looking for a home. And my little buddy Swampy might like to have a friend, especially a female friend. Still concerned that Swampy might run off with her, I made Swampy stay in the house again that night.

Early the next morning I walked over by the outhouse, and put a plate of dog food and a water bowl filled with fresh water on the ground nearby. I took Swampy to work with me again that day.

The first thing I did when we arrived home that evening was to check and see if the dog food had been eaten. The food bowl was empty, and so was the water bowl. Our first step towards making friends had been successfully taken.

I kept Swampy in the house again that night. About ten o'clock I heard Skeeter let out a loud and frantic meow!

Grabbing a flashlight, I ran outside. Her sound was coming from up in the big live oak tree in our front yard. I shined my light on her. My little calico cat was up there on the first branch still meowing her head off.[4]

Not knowing what had her so spooked, I began searching the yard with my flashlight. Upon hearing something move over by the wood pile, I quickly shined my light that way. The first thing I saw was a pair of green eyes looking in my direction. And right away

I knew what was causing all the commotion. That wild German shepherd dog was standing there in our yard! With its tail between its legs, it was shaking slightly, and staring straight at me. To my knowledge, that was the first time, it had ventured into our yard. It was now more evident than ever that it wanted to make friends, but it just wasn't sure how to go about it. Neither was I!

Several days went by. Skeeter had been up and down in that tree countless times. The night time wailing had ceased, but I still kept swampy in the house, and took him to work with me.

Each day I placed food and water by the outhouse. And each night when I came home it was gone. At night, after dark, that wild dog would show up in our yard, and I would go outside and try to make friends with it.

I had decided that if we did make friends, I would name her 'Suwanee', after the famous Suwanee River.[5]

I was hoping it would learn that I meant it no harm, and it was safe to take food from my hand. Several days went by, and finally on the night before my day off at the park, the efforts on the part of both of us began to pay off. She had come into the yard as usual. Skeeter was up in the tree meowing as usual. I walked over to Suwanee, speaking in as soft a tone of voice as I could. In my hand was a slice of fresh and raw deer meat. She was making a whining sound, but this time she did not run away. She stayed right where she was. Slowly I knelt down in front of her, and gently offered her the meat. In as quiet and soothing tone as I could master, I was saying,

"Come on girl. You know you know you love deer meat. Come on take it!"

She hesitated for a moment, and then ever so cautiously, she leaned forward as if to take it. But she didn't. Looking hungrily at the meat, she pulled her head back. I kept on, in a soothing voice, almost begging her to take it.

Finally, with her eyes on mine, she leaned toward my outstretched hand, and this time she ever so gently took the meat in her jaws! As she rushed away from me, in her hunger, she was

"Swampwise"

already eagerly chewing on it. She stopped by the outhouse, and I watched her quickly gobble it down!

She had stopped her whining, and now she was wagging her tail. It was as if she was finally relieved of her burden! And so was I! I slowly walked to the outhouse, and knelt down again. I moved my hand towards her and patted her on the top of her head. Encouraged by her allowing me to do that, I began to stroke her back. Amazingly enough, she did not growl or move away. She seemed to welcome it! And I was thrilled when she started to lick my elbow. I knew we were going to be friends! We stayed there a good while, me stroking her back, and her wagging her tail. Both of us were in a relaxed and friendly mood, just making friends.

She followed me to the front porch. Swampy was inside the house. I could hear him barking anxiously, but I felt it was too soon to let him out with the shepherd.

I put her food dish and her water bowl on the far side of the porch, away from Swampy's and Skeeter's bowls. As I went into the house to calm Swampy down, I noticed that Skeeter had stopped her frantic meowing, but she was still up in that tree.

Off and on all night I heard Swampy whining and scratching at the door, but I would not let him out. Not yet anyhow. We did not hear even a peep from Suwanee.

The next morning I decided it was time for Swampy to meet our new family member. I walked outside with him anxious to see what would happen when they met. I noticed that Skeeter was no longer up in that tree, but I could not be sure where she was.

The meeting was calm and casual. Both Swampy and the shepherd were wagging their tails, sniffing each other all over, just making friends the way most dogs do. Then they began to play dog games, and chase each other all over the front yard. I was relieved to know that things were good between them.

Eventually Skeeter, too, would begin to tolerate our newest member, and we became a happy family! But as we shall see it would not last long.

Okefenokee Joe

Notes:

[1] Living alone in the swamp, by now my ears had become acutely attuned to the sound of any possible danger.
[2] Depending on what he was barking at, there were distinct different tones, and accents in Swampy's bark. I could usually tell by the sound, what he was barking at. He had a special, what I called, 'people bark', which to me was more important than all the others. Out in the swamp the wild animals are predictable. Humans are not!
[3] I always kept my loaded 30 30 Winchester rifle in a rack above the fireplace with a live round in the chamber. I would warn my visitors not to touch the weapon, because it was ready to fire. Often I was asked if it was because of the bears and alligators. Of course, I would answer "No!" The only animals we needed to beware of out there are the human ones!
[4] Skeeter had been spending many a night, during the previous winter, sleeping under the house enjoying the warmth of the brick fire place foundation.
[5] The Okefenokee Swamp is the head waters of the famous Suwanee River which flows from the swamp in Georgia into North Florida.

Part 2: Snake Hunting with Suwanee

Not long after Suwanee had become part of our family I took her with me to a small island off the coast of Georgia to hunt rattlesnakes. I was hoping that I could teach her how to help me find them. Swampy never did quite understand how to do that, and I was constantly concerned about his welfare when I took him on hunts with me.

I had learned through experience that these uninhabited islands were by far the best places in Georgia to find the largest and most healthy specimens of the eastern diamondback rattlesnake![1]

The particular island I had in mind was located just off the coast, near what is now a nuclear submarine base. Back then it was an Army supply Depot. I had already taken a great number of snakes off of it.

"Swampwise"

From the landing at Crooked River State Park, it took about twenty minutes to get there. At low tide, there were about a hundred yards of mud and muck between it and the water. It was all but impossible to get a boat up close to the island at low tide.

I had planned our trip so that it would be high tide when we would arrive at our destination. At high tide the island would be surrounded by water, and we could easily pull up close to it.

When we got there, the tide was not yet high. I drove the boat up into the soft mud of the marsh, and turned off the engine. I was busy getting my hunting gear together, when Suwanee surprised me by jumping out of the boat. I did not see her do it. I heard her do it. When I looked over at her, and saw what had happened to her, it almost made me laugh! But I didn't! Her feet, all four of them had sunk deep into the muck up to her shoulders! She couldn't move. It was a comical sight, but a serious predicament she was in! I wasn't quite sure how to get her out of it! If I jumped in to help her, I would sink into the muck too. She had begun to whine, and I knew I must do something!

I started the motor again, took a chance, and drove the boat further into the muck. I was closer to her now, and I could reach her from the boat. I grabbed her with both hands, and pulled her back into the boat. She was filthy, but she was safe.

There were oyster clutches and piles of sea shells scattered around the area, and I had long since learned that I could walk on most of them without sinking. I was not sure that I could teach that to Suwanee, but I knew I must give it a try. So I got out of the boat and standing on a clutch of oysters, I called to Suwanee, "Come here!"

She jumped out of the boat, and landed on the same clutch where I was! She did not sink in the muck. I moved to the next clutch, then to the next, and she followed me. Problem solved! We were on the island, and the hunt began.

My snake hunting equipment consisted of a snake hook, a little hand mirror, and an old surplus army gas mask bag tied around my waist, full of empty cloth snake bags.[2]

I had hoped that Suwanee would stay by my side as we walked

along. But she didn't. She was off into the bush the moment we arrived on dry land. Apparently she had already found something, because he started barking. I couldn't see her, so I moved in the direction of her barking, hoping it was a rattler that had her attention.

I found her barking at an armadillo burrow, surrounded by thick clumps of wire grass, next to a small live oak tree. By the way she was acting I knew that something was in there. She looked over at me when I arrived on the scene, and she increased the tone of her barking. I watched her put her nose into the opening of the burrow, and I thought to myself, "Please don't do that! There very well could be a rattlesnake in there!"[3]

I did not realize it at that moment, but I was about to learn something about armadillo hunting. Suwanee would teach me! She shoved her nose deeper into the burrow, and it was obvious that she had grabbed a hold of something, and was yanking and pulling at it roughly! She did that for several minutes! Then she did something that thoroughly amazed me! Suddenly, instead of pulling, she began pushing violently at her quarry! Immediately she pulled her head out of the burrow, and in her jaws was a very surprised screaming, and struggling adult armadillo!

Suwanee had taught me an easy way to catch an armadillo! As if I'll ever want to catch one! Apparently Suwanee had learned that if she pulled on it, it would pull back. And if she pushed on it, it was just stupid enough to push back. A simple trick, but it sure made it easy to get an armadillo out of its burrow.

I watched her play with it for a little while, but it just stayed rolled up in a ball, and she soon lost interest in it. It was time to move on anyhow. I'll never forget that lesson she taught me.

I found my first snake coiled up, sunning itself next to a fallen Palmetto log. It was a Diamondback! About a four footer, and it was sound asleep. Until it felt me gently pin its head down, the snake did not even know I was there. I grabbed it behind its head, and picked it up. With my other hand I quickly grabbed it in the middle of its body to keep it from wriggling out of my grasp! It did not fully wake up and rattle until I had it safely tucked away in a snake bag. That was an easy catch![4]

Suwanee disappeared again, and I had not seen her or heard her for quite a while. In the meantime I had bagged two more fairly large deadly, but beautiful Diamondbacks. They were lying close together just outside an old rusty half buried irrigation pipe. Like the first one I caught, I had taken them both by surprise. Believe me they are much easier to catch that way. If they are already riled up and rattling, it is sometimes very difficult to catch them without hurting them, or them hurting us!

I could hear Suwanee barking way off in the distance, and I hurried over to see what she had going on this time. When I found her, she had a welcome surprise for me, and it made me glad I had brought her with me.

She had two diamondbacks cornered for me. She had been holding them at bay by walking around them, in the same manner that I had seen Skeeter the cat do months before. She was smart enough to move away when I got there, and I began the chore of capturing them. They were, by now, both very much awake, and alert. Apparently they were far from any cover, because they were both coiled, rattling, and standing their ground![5]

With my snake hook, I very carefully lifted one of them off the ground, and placed it a safe distance from the other. I did that because they were so close together I would be unable to catch one without being bitten by the other. They both stayed where they were, and I was able to safely get them both into a bag as I had done previously with the others. By the end of the hunt we had captured seven eastern diamondback rattlesnakes. It had been a good hunt, and I was glad I had taken Suwanee with me. She had been a real help.

Notes:

[1] Because not many humans visit these islands the rattlesnakes are able to live longer, and grow bigger!

[2] On one end of the snake hook I carried was an L shaped, half inch piece of iron rod sharpened at its end. That end of it was used to rip up old stumps, and lift up logs or other snake cover. On the other end was an L shaped iron rod with a round end that was used to lift the snake up, or to pin its head down.

[3] I had learned that rattlesnakes seeking shelter seem to prefer vacant burrows, uninhabited by the animal that had dug them. But occasionally they will make use of one that is inhabited. So when we hunt we usually check them all.

[4] It has been my experience that rattlesnakes spend about seventy percent of their time sleeping. They cannot close their eyes to show us that they are asleep, but if that snake has not moved, flickered its tongue or done something to let us know that it is aware of us, without pinning its head down, we can actually reach down, and grab it behind its head, and pick it up. But a person should never try doing that without first learning it from an expert!

[5] If a rattlesnake is in strange territory, and not sure where the nearest shelter is, invariably it will choose to stand its ground and face the intruder no matter what the odds! I've seen big ones stop right in the middle of a dirt road, coil up, and face an oncoming pickup truck! It will not run. But it should be noted that it also most definitely will not attack!

Part 3: The Dastardly Deed

When dogs run in a pack they tend to do things they would never dream of doing if they were alone. Such was the case with Swampy and Suwanee. Now that there were two dogs instead of one, they had become a pack. In a way that was fun for all of us, but as it turned out, there were some serious consequences.

Out at the park I was caring for eleven captive Virginia whitetail deer. They were on exhibit in a natural habitat compound behind what was known as the Interpretive Center. It was about an acre in size. An eight foot tall fence, with two strands of electric barbed wire fence strung above it, surrounded the compound. Visitors at the park could watch the deer through a large picture glass window in the lobby of the building. There were benches supplied for them, and they were welcome to sit, and stay as long as they wished.

For months before the arrival of Suwanee, Swampy would stay in the yard at night. He seldom roamed, and I was thankful for that, because there were several species of predatory animals out in that swamp that would have loved to catch him and devour him. But when Suwanee became a member of our little family, life changed. My two domestic dogs had become a pack. They began to roam, and stay gone for hours at a time. I had no idea where they were or what they were up to. I tried not to be too concerned about it, but I couldn't help it, I was concerned. I was hoping nothing drastic would happen.

One night they were gone until the wee hours of the morning. I had called to them often during the evening hours. Still wondering where they were, I finally went to bed.

I was awakened when I heard them drinking from their water bowls on the porch. I looked over at my luminous clock. It was three a. m. I got out of bed, and went out on the porch to see if they were okay.

They both looked ragged and worn out, and both water bowls were empty. I filled their bowls up again and looked them over thoroughly, finding nothing visibly wrong with them, I went back to bed. I remember falling asleep wondering where they had been.

When I left for the park the next morning, they stayed on the porch and watched me drive away. Usually they would follow me a little ways, barking. But this time they didn't do that. They were really worn out, and they just laid there.

When I got to the park, I began my daily rounds, checking on all the critters under my care. The bears where fine, the gators were all accounted for, and my river otters looked happy. Everything was looking good, until I arrived at the deer compound, and looked out at the deer. Disaster had struck! The shock of that dreadful scene went through me like a lightning bolt! I thought,

"What in the world? How could this have happened?"

Two of our prize deer were lying dead on the ground, both of them torn to pieces! I ran out into the compound, and found another one by the back gate, in the same condition. And there was another one on the far end, bleeding, and limping badly! What a dreadful sight, and what a problem I suddenly had on my hands! What could possibly have done this?

Looking for a clue, as to what might have committed this horrible crime, I frantically started looking for tracks. But there had been too much action in the compound, and all the tracks in the area had been destroyed beyond recognition. I decided to walk the perimeter, and look for any evidence of illegal entry.

I had gone almost completely around the fence, when I came to the clue I was looking for. There it was, right before my eyes! A pile of fresh dirt, and next to it lay the evidence! A deep hole! Something had dug a hole under the fence!

I looked around for tracks or any sign that would prove what it was but there had been so much traffic on the ground all around the hole that all tracks there were also indistinguishable. I went back into the compound, and looked again for tracks. I finally found some over by the pond!

To my disbelief, they were canine tracks!

Putting two and two together, I realized who the culprits must have been. My 'pack' must have been here! Totally dismayed at that realization, I ran to the parking lot, jumped in my jeep, and hurriedly drove the one mile to my house.

Swampy and Suwanee were sound asleep on the porch when I drove up. They both jumped up to greet me, but I was already greeting them with shouts of disapproval, and reprimand! It was difficult to believe that they had done that atrocious deed! Especially Swampy! He did not have a cruel bone in his body!

Of course, neither one of them knew what I was raving about. And I'm sure that all my shouting had them both very much confused. But I was so disappointed in them that if I'd let myself, I probably could have cried.

Then I got to thinking. Maybe Swampy didn't do it! Maybe Swampy wasn't even there! Maybe Suwanee did it all! She was the breed of dog that could be vicious enough to do it without Swampy. I had to be sure! I needed proof!

Suddenly an idea came to me. I would take Swampy by himself out to the park, and see if he could show me where the hole was. I figured if he knew where it was, he must have been in on that horrible escapade.

Swampy and a deeply worried me, arrived at the deer compound, and I allowed Swampy to roam free. The second I did that, he ran straight to the hole in the fence, and proceeded to enter the compound! I, of course stopped him. But now, sadly enough I knew that he had been a part of that dastardly deed. He had just proven it to me! He knew where the hole under the fence was!

I took him home, and chained him up in the yard. I did the same to Suwanee. I was taking no chances of a repeat performance. I went back out to the park, and thank goodness I was able to remove the dead bodies, clean up the mess, and get the wounded deer to the vet, all before the visitors began to arrive. Nobody saw it! No one even knew that it had even happened! Nobody but me!

I knew I must get rid of Suwanee! I was so upset I did not take time out for lunch with my coworkers. I drove home, grabbed my twenty-two rifle, put Suwanee on her leash, and all but threw her in the jeep! I drove as fast as I could to the trash dump. I had every intention of executing Suwanee. She was bad, and I knew there was no way I could change her ways. And as long as she was around, she would influence Swampy into doing things Swampy would never do alone. At the trash dump, with my rifle pointing at her head, and Suwanee looking up at me innocently, I began to pull the trigger. But just at that moment I heard the honking sound of the horn of a pickup truck coming up the road! A moment later it pulled up beside us, and the driver hollered,

"Wait a minute! Don't do that! I want that dog!"

It was one of my co-workers. Somehow he had heard about what I planned to do with Suwanee. He had seen her several times, and he liked her. She seemed to like him too. I told the man he could have Suwanee under one condition. She must never be allowed near the swamp again. Of course he agreed! He put her in the truck with him, and happily drove off! So Suwanee was saved by the bell, or better said, "By the truck horn"! She had a new home, and my co-worker friend had a new friend. I never saw Suwanee again. All is well that ends well!

For the rest of his short life, Swampy seldom ventured far from home. He and I had many wonderful and unforgettable adventures living there on Cowhouse Island in the great Okefenokee Swamp! We were Swampwise! And we loved it!

CHAPTER 5
STREAK THE BOBCAT

Part 1: Making Friends

I don't care much for house cats. To me, they don't make really good pets. Most of them are too independent. They seldom come to you when you call them, and they only accept your love for them on their own terms. Some people appreciate that. But I don't. There were only two cats that I really cared for. Only two cats I ever really loved. One of course was "Skeeter", my little calico house cat. The other I named "Streak". He was supposed to be independent. He was born that way. He wasn't bred to recognize a human as his master. That cat wasn't meant to be, and shouldn't be expected to be somebody's pet. He was a full blown, two month old male, truly wild bobcat kitten, handed to me by the Georgia State Game Commission in the Okefenokee Swamp. I was to care for him, and when the time came, to place him on exhibit at the Park. The former I would gladly do. The latter, well, from the very beginning, Streak and me had different plans.

    For the first several weeks he had no name. I wanted to know him better, before I gave him a proper name, one that actually would fit his personality.

    He was a beautiful healthy kitten, and a perfect replica of his parents. Like all youngsters of his age (even wild ones) he seemed to welcome love, care, and guidance. From the animals of the swamp themselves I was learning that, although wild animals are born with instinctive knowledge and survival skills, there are invariably many things that they must learn through experience, and to become fully skilled they must practice.

If a wild animal survives through the first year of its life without mishap, it usually means it has learned most of what it needs to know to go on living. Such are the ways of the creatures of the swamp. And as we shall see, Streak was no exception to that rule.

I made a pact with him in the very beginning. I felt that, just like me, the Great Okefenokee Swamp was his back yard. The Indians called it, "The Land of the Trembling Earth". It is huge! It covers more than seven hundred and fifty square miles of mostly pristine wilderness, dotted with many uninhabited islands, and located in deep Southeastern Georgia. The swamp belonged to him, and he belonged to it. And I promised him that anytime he wanted to go out there and be a real bobcat, as far as I was concerned, he was free to do so. Of course, I told that to no one else. It was our secret, and we kept it that way.

In order to gain his trust I made it a point to be consistent in all my dealings with him. For example, I made sure that I always approached his enclosure from the same direction, and I always talked to him, and let him know I was coming. And every time I was leaving him for any length of time I would always say the words "See you later"! And he knew not to expect me back for some time. When I said, "Chop, chop," he understood that food was coming. If I said, "Go for it," he knew he had my permission to act on his own. As he grew older, the "Go for it" phrase was no longer needed or used. For the first few weeks, though, he acted as if he needed my support, and my guidance.

I purposely spoke very little around him or to him, in hopes that the few things I did say he would come to understand. As it turned out, he was a fast learner. I too was a fast learner!

Almost immediately I discovered that there were two things I must never do. One was never offer to feed him by hand. His primeval reaction to the mere sight or smell of food would cause him to viciously make sure, at all costs, he'd get his share. Several times his hunger caused such eagerness in him that he all but devoured my left hand. And although he seemed to like being held and loved, I found out the hard way that I must never hold him close and expose my bare neck to him. The results could be painful, if not fatal.

The one and only time I mistakenly did that he quickly seized the opportunity to sink his teeth into my neck. Thank goodness he did not proceed to chew or slash! Suddenly realizing that he had made a mistake, he let go of my neck. That, by the way, is how I learned that because of their inherent instinct to survive, carnivores will sometimes take immediate and fierce advantage of any situation that might give them the upper hand. Such are the ways of all creatures in the forest. And again this cat was no exception to the rule.

Out in back of the park, where the tourists were prohibited, we constructed a 6' x 10' x 6' wooden enclosure with a water proof roof to keep out the rain. I built a platform with a hide box high up near the back of it, hoping he'd feel more secure and at home up in that corner. It seemed to suit him just fine because he spent most of his time in the hide box. He always had a water bowl with fresh water. After a day or two of living in his new abode, he seemed accustomed to his surroundings, and I believe he really liked it there.

Twice a day we would take a thirty minute walk about in the beautiful dense forest behind the park. We did this without a leash. The cat never was forced to wear a collar. To me he was more of a friend than a pet. On all of our excursions he was free to come and go on his own. In the very beginning he would stay by my side, or close at my heels, seldom venturing very far from me.

While he was learning to be a bobcat, I was learning from him about bobcats. This seemed to me, and probably to him, as a fair exchange. I could see this as further truth that when wild animals are young they do need guidance, and at least some affection.

After several weeks of our twice-a-day excursions, little by little Streak began to wander off on his own. At first he would take short trips, never getting out of sight or hearing from me. To make sure he would know exactly where I was, in a soothing voice, I used these same two phrases over and over,

"Where is that cat? Where can he be worries me", and "Some kinda' cat I'll tell you that!"

As mentioned earlier, to avoid confusion in his tiny precious mind, I always used short words or phrases, and seldom ever said anything else in his presence.

Each day, on all of our walk abouts I carried a field guide to the plants of the Southeastern United States with me. I used it frequently to help familiarize myself with the vegetation of the Okefenokee Swamp.

Streak's power of association was phenomenal. I believe it was keener than that of most German shepherd dogs. On each of our walk abouts, I made it our habit to stop for a moment at certain locations along the way. I had given names to each of these spots, and Streak was quick to learn those names. For example I would say, "Pine Cone Playground", or, "Gopher Hole!"

And sometimes he'd be there before me, and sometimes he'd linger elsewhere, but eventually he'd always arrive. This action on his part is what led me to believe that he really enjoyed our games.

The "Pine Cone Playground" was one of the many spots we'd visit twice a day on our short learning trips. As a matter of fact it became famous to us, because it's the place where Streak earned his name!

He seemed to enjoy our walks as much, if not more, than I did. One day I said, "Pine Cone Playground!"

And I proceeded on my way to that spot. As usual, Streak was there waiting for me, and he was ready to play the pine cone game.

We kept a small pile of Slash Pine cones in between two large trees. I'd say, "Catch!" and roll one across the ground. Streak would grab it in his front paws, play with it a while, then toss it around just like a domestic kitten.

After several days of this game, I began to toss the pine cone a little higher, sometimes forcing him to jump off the ground to catch it. He seemed to love doing that, and we'd play with about six pine cones on each trip.

"Swampwise"

Then one day, just to see what might happen, I threw a pine cone a little higher, about five feet off the ground. What happened next totally amazed me! What a fantastic surprise!

Faster than lightning Streak jumped up the full five feet off the ground, took the pine cone in his front paws, shoved it into his mouth, jumped to a nearby tree, sunk his claws into the tree, and hung there on the side of the tree! He accomplished all of that in what seemed to be one movement! What a thrill it was to see my little friend do that! I felt so proud of him, and I believe he knew it. I reached up and pulled him off that little tree he stayed perched on my shoulder all the way back to his enclosure! That was an important day for us. That's the day my little furry bobcat friend earned his name!

"He was faster than lightning, so I called him Streak"![2]

Notes:

[1] The exact translation of the combination of Creek Indian words O KE FE NO KE is "Water with no feet." That was their way of interpreting the decaying vegetation floating to the top of the water, and gradually through the years becoming a semi solid mass floating in the water.

[2] Excerpt from Joe's song "Streak the bobcat".

Foot Note: A cat can see movement at a great distance, and because of its intense curiosity, it will often be attracted to it. Nuisance animal trappers know this, and they often tie a bright feather, or some other shiny and light object that will move in the wind, above or near their traps, when they are after cats.

Part 2: The Learning Process

I made it a point on our twice a day jaunts, to give fairly simple names to our meeting places. The "Crooked Tree," the "Gopher Hole," the "Cypress Stump" were the names of a few of them. Just as he did with 'The Pine Cone Playground', he came to understand where to meet me. Sometimes, while I was on my way to the spot I had called out, he would lie in wait and ambush me. That was fun, but also very painful for me.

Although I was aware of where he was, and that he was sneaking up on me, I pretended to act surprised when he would spring to the attack, and jump on my back. I recall many a time the need for someone to apply iodine to the cuts in my back.

His claws were so long and razor sharp that they would pierce all the way through even my thickest wool jacket, and sink into my back! That's when I came to realize that he needed a bobcat, or some other kind of furry creature to play that game. We humans, with no fur on our bodies, are sissies compared to our wild animal 'neighbors'!

The "Cypress Stump" was a stump about two feet high. Its top had been sawed flat. I was able to comfortably sit down upon it. The first time I did that, Streak taught me another lesson. He came up to me purring like a kitten, and he began rubbing his chin on my knee. I soon found out that when he was in that mood, I could pet him, and actually hug him.

At times I would also hear him meow just like a domestic cat. Never the less I realized that he was truly a wild animal, and as such was not meant to be someone's house pet.

The sounds mentioned above are all sounds of contentment, and mean no ill intent. There are many other sounds that bobcats make. We will talk about some of those sounds, and their meaning, as time goes by.[1]

Along our trail we found a pine tree that had been stunted in its early years. It was about seven feet tall, its branches were stretched out close to the ground and they were crooked and twisted. We named it "The Crooked Tree." This is where Streak began to learn how to climb a tree.

Yes, believe it or not, although they are born with many inherent instincts, I was seeing with my own eyes, that even bobcats must learn certain survival skills. Tree climbing did not come easy to Streak the cat. Perhaps if his momma had been with him, she could have shown him quickly, how to climb. But his momma was not with him. All he had was me.

At first he was reluctant to climb any higher than my shoulder. As time went on, as we shall see, although it took time, patience, and practice, Streak did eventually learn to climb.

It is a well-known fact that all members of the cat family have what is referred to as retractable claws, which means cats have the ability to retract their claws and keep them hidden. In other words, they can paw at things without using their claws. They spring their claws into play only when they need them.[2]

Sometimes, when Streak was in a playful mood, he'd roll over on his back, and I'd scratch and tickle his belly. That was always fun for a while, because he would bite my hands gently, and happily paw at my forearms without using his claws.

But invariably he would get so excited that he would forget his manners, and begin to bite harder, and use his claws instead of his paws. That hurt! And we would have to quit the game. I was forever walking around with deep cat scratches and cuts in my hands and forearms.

These days with Streak were a true blessing for me. I was receiving an education that no book on earth could provide. I was learning the truth about bobcats, first hand, from Streak himself.

It is said that, "In many things, experience is the best teacher", and I totally agree. My experiences with Streak were living proof for me, that the saying is true. He was definitely helping me to become "Swampwise!"

A great deal of my time was spent studying and trying to make sense of what I had seen Streak do each day. I had time to do that because I lived by myself in the swamp, and I had no one else to occupy my time. I was alone, but because of the animals I was caring for, I was not often lonely, just sometimes.

Once a day, in the late afternoon, I fed him a small mixture of dry cat food mixed with canned cat food. His water bowl was always filled with fresh water. Several weeks down the road when he started to bring rats, mice and squirrels to show me, I began to feed him raw meat, small chickens, and the whole bodies of rats, mice, squirrels, and fresh fish.

Because he would become so uncontrollable around food, I found that I must make sure he was back in his enclosure before I brought out his fresh meat dinner. I had cut a slit in the bottom of his door, just large enough to slip the food bowl in. From that time on that's how Streak was fed.

Notes:

[1] Sometimes, late at night, I would hear a mournful wailing sound emanating from the bear compound. It was the huge male bobcat we had on exhibit in there. It was not a scream, like that of a panther. It did not even sound like a cat. I do not know what it meant.

[2] This is also one way to distinguish cat tracks from those of other furry creatures. Cats leave tracks with no claw marks.

Part 3: The School Bus Encounter

One morning, just after I had brought Streak out of his wooden enclosure for our walk about, a huge school bus full of happy screaming kids drove by. This was totally unexpected because usually there was no traffic out in back of the park.

The sound and the sight of the bus terrified my little friend, and in his panic he dashed off deep into the forest. This was only about a week after he had been delivered into my care. We really had not yet had enough time to become truly familiar with each other. That worried me deeply, because I was growing attached to him, and I most surely did not want to lose him.

When the dust from the wheels of the school bus finally dissipated, and the roar of its engine had subsided, I walked into the woods in the direction he had gone, and began calling out his name. Again and again I called for him. Again and again there was no answer. I tried for almost an hour searching and calling for him. Finally, the time came when I had to leave the area and give a wildlife presentation in the lecture room at the park. Temporarily I was forced to leave Streak to his own devices.

With Streak weighing desperately on my mind, I struggled through my lecture. I don't remember much of what I said, and I cut the question and answer session short.

Then I was back outside again calling for Streak. Still there was no answer. I kept looking for him until the park closed, and I had to leave. As darkness approached, I was more worried than ever. I was so afraid that I might have lost him forever. I was also thinking, "Darn that school bus!" I decided to forego supper, and go back out to the park, and look for him again.

With the top down on my 1973 Volkswagen Thing, which I affectionately called "my Jeep," and Swampy sitting beside me, I drove on back out the park. I am glad that Swampy went with me!

I parked out in back of the park, near the spot where I had last seen Streak, turned off the engine, and listened. All the usual springtime night sounds of the swamp are such sweet music to my ears. The tiny, Southern Peeper Frogs, the crickets, an occasional Narrow mouthed Toad, a Pig Frog, a Barred Owl, or the distant sound of a gator bellowing—all of these—were what I call "The sounds of freedom". I was hearing my favorite songs, but I heard no sound from Streak.

Diligently, but unsuccessfully I called his name, and searched the underbrush all around the area for better than an hour with no sound from Streak. Deciding sadly that he was probably gone forever, I called it quits, got back in the jeep, and started the engine.

I had driven only about twenty yards when Swampy started barking excitedly. He was looking off to the right at the underbrush on the side of the road. I stopped the jeep immediately, turned off the engine, and listened. All I could hear was Swampy's barking.

I quickly got out of the jeep, and with my headlamp turned on, I began frantically searching in the nearby bushes. Then, even with Swampy's loud barking, I thought I heard a most welcome and familiar sound. I listened more closely, and sure enough there it was! I was hearing an ever so faint meow coming from behind the trunk of a fallen slash pine tree!

I shined my light over the fallen tree, and there he was! I immediately felt tremendous relief! *Thank God*! I had found my little friend!

I was so happy to see Streak again! He seemed to feel the same way, because he began purring in my arms, as I carried him back to his enclosure. I'll never know why he did not answer me, or come back to me during all that time I was hunting for him. But it didn't matter now. He was back now. And he was home now!

I rewarded Swampy that evening by giving him extra hugs. I was so thankful that my little bobcat cat was safe that I also gave Swampy my supper. The supper that I had hurriedly foregone because of my concern over Streak. It was a delicious, medium rare one and a half pound T-bone steak. It was cold now, but Swampy loved it! Gratefully wagging his tail, he took it, and gobbled it down bone and all. My supper was simply a bowl of cereal. Streak was safe, and things were good!

Part 4: "Kee Yote" The Bobcat

In the lobby of our serpentarium, through a large picture glass window, visitors could safely observe the several American black bears that we had on exhibit. They were housed in a large natural habitat enclosure, surrounded by an electric fence, which kept them within eyesight of our visitors. The fence was disguised so that the public could not see it. The bears certainly knew it was there, and we had no bear escapes, ever.

On exhibit, along with the bears, we also kept a huge male bobcat. We had named it Kee Yote. It had been confiscated, and brought to the park by the Georgia State Game Commission several years before. At the time I was given the job of curator of animals at the park, Kee Yote was on exhibit in a ten by ten foot iron barred chain link enclosure.

The poor cat had its teeth, but it had no claws. Apparently, who ever had it in their possession, was attempting to make it their house pet. It was obvious that their plan could never work, because this cat was already an adult, and just as wild as a bobcat can be.

I could not make friends with it. I tried to act gently, offer it food, and speak to it with the most comforting voice I could muster. But at my mere presence it would cower in the back corner of its cage, and hiss and snarl at me. Once it was so upset over the sight of me, that it actually regurgitated its last meal!

Oddly enough though, I learned that each day, when it was time to clean its cage, it would allow me to enter, and wash the cement floor with a water hose. It would stay in the corner with its back and its hair up, snarling at me, fearfully watching every move I made, but it would not attack me. I could walk all around its cage, talk to it, and clean out its water and food bowls, and it would not come near me.

The attitude it would display though made it clear to me, that the one thing I must not do, is get close to it, and try to pet it. I knew that it would not allow me to touch it. But the most important thing I learned about its attitude towards me is that under no circumstances would it attack me.

That's when I began to understand that creatures of the wild will attack, with intent to kill only what they plan on eating. Believe it or not, I found this to be true with all forms of life in the natural world, including snakes!

I am sure that my odor and the mere sight of me was most displeasing and unappetizing to the cat. Besides that, although the cat might not know what I was, it certainly knew I was much too big to tangle with or to eat. It wanted absolutely nothing to do with me which led me to another enlightening observation.

Wild animals do not wish to be our close friends. But they also do not wish to be our enemies. All of them are meant to be left alone, without any interference from the human race. Each and every one of them is performing the duties that *God* has created them to do for the health and welfare of Planet Earth. The only game any wild creature would be willing to play with a human is a game called *Live and Let Live*.

The powers that be at the park knew that without claws, the cat's chances of survival in the wild were slim. It would be unfair to the cat to turn it loose in the swamp. The park's decision was to place the cat on exhibit in the natural habitat of the American black bear Compound, along with the bears. That way, with more freedom and room to move about, at least it would be more comfortable.

Each evening, at feeding time, I would go out there and try to call him up. Sometimes he would come, sometimes he wouldn't. When that was the case, I just left his warm, fresh, raw chicken, fish, or beef dinner out there, away from the reach of the bears, where he would eventually find it. Often, to make sure he received all the nutrients he needed, I would give him a whole rabbit, or rat. It was very difficult, if not impossible, to take proper care of that poor cat.

Part 5: Streak Meets Kee Yote

A month or so, after streak arrived in my care, he met Kee Yote face to face. And this is how it happened.

For over a week now, I had been trying to get Streak to climb. I would hold him close to a trunk of a tree until his claws dug into the bark, and he could stay there by himself. But he was reluctant to climb on up the tree. He seemed to prefer being down from the tree rather than on up in the tree. I was greatly puzzled by this, because, after all, he was a natural born wild animal, and a cat at that. Even house cats love to climb trees. Don't they?

Well, one afternoon, after a failed attempt at tree climbing, as we were returning from a walk about, he suddenly veered away from me. He was headed squarely in the direction of the bear compound. Before I could stop him, he had climbed under the fence, and was inside the compound. I never dreamed that he would do something like that. I didn't think he could do something like that. But he was just tiny enough to fit under that fence. And there he was, in the compound with the bears, and also that huge male bobcat named Kee Yote![1]

In a split second, to my further dismay, Kee Yote had pounced upon the scene! They both must have somehow been aware of each other's presence, and what happened next was a truly awesome, once in a life time, learning experience for me.

I witnessed a lone, young orphaned male bobcat meeting, for the first time in its life, a huge, unfriendly, and seemingly vicious, adult male bobcat, four times its size. Fearing for Streak's safety, and not sure what I could do about it, I watched this scene from outside the bear compound. I was about twenty feet away, and feeling helpless.

Kee Yote, baring his teeth, and omitting a fierce, threatening, hissing "cat growl", obviously had the upper hand. He stood, towering menacingly over my poor little frightened friend, with his ears back, his hair straight up, and with his bobbed tail straight out, moving in a jerking motion!

Streak, on the other hand, had immediately assumed a completely submissive attitude. Rolling over on his back, with all four paws in the air, hiding his claws, just showing his paws he began uttering a faint, high pitched growling sound. It was an almost human-like prayer meaning, "I'm a bobcat, too. I just want to be friends. Please don't hurt me!"

Kee Yote stood over him growling in that horrific menacing manner for several minutes. Then he backed away. From where I stood, I could still hear his ominous, hissing "cat growl".

As the big cat began to move away, Streak, without a sound, immediately stood up again on all four legs. Upon seeing this, Kee Yote quickly returned and towered over him again!

He began exhibiting that same terrible threatening manner he had displayed earlier. Streak again went back into total submission, lying on his back, this time making a kitten like, whining sound. This scenario was repeated over and over again for about fifteen minutes.

Then suddenly, as the huge cat was moving away, Streak stood up, and made a break for the nearest tree. It was a Long Leaf Pine, about two feet in diameter, and Streak did not just climb it, he seemed to run up it. Lo and behold, for the first time in his life my tiny orphaned friend had climbed a tree.[2]

Thank God Kee Yote had no claws, and could not climb up after him. Perhaps a wild bobcat, with claws would have followed Streak right on up that tree. We'll never know about that. But Kee Yote had no claws and Streak was safe, at least for now.

Kee Yote pawed at the trunk of the tree over and over again, as if to start climbing it. Without his claws though, he was unable to do it. He settled for pacing around the tree, uttering those low-pitched and menacing "cat growls." Then, finally with his eyes on Streak, he laid down not far from the tree. He seemed to settle down there, waiting, demonstrating that eternal patience known and possessed only by the members of the wild animal kingdom.[3]

I imagine Streak was feeling temporarily safe from that monster. But now, another serious, unforeseen problem arose, and we had come to another lesson in my little orphaned friend's life.

Notes:

[1] It was obvious that Streak had what seemed to be an uncontrollable desire to be with his own kind.
[2] During the whole scene Kee Yote never once touched Streak or harmed him in any way, except to frighten him
[3] In the winter time when the leaves of the hardwoods have fallen, it is easy to see birds of prey of all breeds waiting in the trees along our modern highways, for 'Road Kill' meals. They do that all year round. It's just difficult to see them waiting there, through the heavier foliage of the warmer months. They will stay perched motionless and silent for hours and

hours. This is just one example of the eternal patience known only to the members of the wild animal kingdom.

Part 6: Tree Climbing 101

When Streak climbed up in that tree it was obvious that he was most certainly terrified of that huge bobcat waiting for him at the bottom. That's one good reason for his staying up there. But, as the hours, and the days went by I learned another, equally, and possibly more important reason why he was still up there.

I went into the bear compound to rescue Streak many times a day, over the next several days. Each time Kee Yote was still keeping his vigil near the tree, watching Streak, and I would chase him away. That was easy to do because that big cat was so fearful of me.

I would call to Streak, using the most comforting sounds I could come up with, telling him he was safe, and he could climb down now. But he would not budge from his perch, about forty feet high, up in that tree. This had me greatly puzzled. Cats are supposed to climb up and down trees. I thought to myself, "Give it time. He's a wild animal. He'll figure it out, and come back down." But he didn't.

Three days went by. Each day I was out there countless times trying to coax him down from that tree. This had become a more serious problem than I had anticipated, and I was extremely concerned about his welfare. I just could not believe it. Could it be that he just did know how to climb back down?

For three full days Streak had had neither water nor food. He might die up there. I decided that I had to climb the tree myself, and try to coax him down.

I entered the bear compound, screaming, "Get back Kee Yote!" at the top of my lungs. I knew the big cat would not come near us. But for Streak's benefit, I kept yelling loudly and forcibly for him to stay away.

I called to Streak, but he would not climb down. I waited several minutes, giving him the chance to come down on his own, but he just would not do it. So I proceeded to climb up the tree after him.

When I was about three feet from him, I looked up at him. I could not be sure whether he was glad to see me or not. His viscous covered eyelids were slightly closed, and with his dry mouth partially open, he was uttering a faint hissing sound. I wasn't sure exactly what that meant. But I was determined to get him out of that tree. I just threw all caution to the wind, and took the chance. I quickly reached up, took him by the nap of his neck, the way his 'momma' would have done, placed him on my shoulder, and slid back down the tree to the ground.

With Streak safe and sound once more, carrying him in my arms, we quickly left the bear compound. Problem solved. At least I thought it was.

This is when I began to understand that just as with climbing up a tree, climbing back down from a tree is something Streak had to learn. It seems that wild animals must sometimes learn through experience. And again apparently Streak was no exception.

I fed him some warm milk, and a small ration of canned cat food. It was his first meal in several days, and I most certainly did not want to overdo it. Each day I fed him a little more, until we were back to his usual daily ration.

Getting back to his climbing problems, I had come up with another plan. I placed him on my shoulder, climbed up a tree, and held him a short distance above me, until he sank his claws into the tree. Then I let go of him. I was about two feet down the trunk from him, and apparently my nearness gave him all the confidence he needed, because immediately he crawled and slid backwards down to me.

I shouted, "Hooray!" placed him on my shoulder, and slid the rest of the way down the tree. Streak had learned what any cat needs to know. He had learned that he could crawl backwards when coming down a tree.

After that, without any help or coaxing from me, Streak began to practice climbing up trees, and climbing back down from them. In less than a week he became an expert. He had also learned that instead of sliding backwards down a tree, he could also walk back down head first!

Then, as he gained confidence, he began to climb higher and higher. He quickly graduated from small saplings to the larger pines. Some of those old mature pine trees were eighty to a hundred and twenty feet tall.

The feats he began performing, while high up in the branches, would just about take my breath away. He would swing like a wild monkey from one branch to another. Sometimes the branch he was holding would break, and as he started to fall, he'd just grab another branch on the way down. He'd use the new branch to swing back to the trunk of the tree, and run, not climb, but run, further up the tree. He'd run out a branch until it bent down with his weight, and then run back the branch to the trunk of the tree. All of this he would do eighty or ninety feet above the ground. Some of his antics would absolutely astonish me, and truly frighten me for his sake.

But he had become an expert, and in such a short time. There were still other important survival skills he must learn. It was a pileated woodpecker that would teach him his next important lesson about trees.[1]

Note:

[1] The notion that wild animals just naturally know what to do to survive is not entirely true. There are many things they must learn, and sometimes other animals help them to do that.

Part 7: Streak Meets the 'Clown of the Forest'

By the end of the second month of our relationship, Streak was fast learning how to be a real bobcat. He could climb up and down the trees, catch his own food, which consisted mostly of rabbits, mice or rats, sometimes a bird, and believe it or not even several times a snake. I saw most of what he was catching, because he would bring his prey to me. I loved it when he did that, because it let me know that we had a good solid understanding relationship.

One afternoon he brought me a very dangerous pygmy rattlesnake. It was still alive. Right in front of me he dropped it on the ground, slapped at it with his paws, took it in his jaws, threw it up in the air, and slapped at it some more on its way down. Then he lay down on top of the snake, and with the snake wriggling under him, he proceeded to rub the fur on his back all over the snake's body.[1]

Obviously he was attempting to mix the odor of its musk into his fur. Many animals, including domestic dogs, do this same procedure with foul smelling carcasses of dead animals.

Watching streak with that little rattlesnake, I was concerned that the snake might bite him. But he seemed to know exactly what he was doing with it. Why cats play with, or better said, "torture" their prey is a mystery to me. No other animal that I know of will do that.

I remember one day, during a question and answer period in the lecture room, I mentioned that fact to my audience. A sweet little cat loving lady stood up and blatantly chastised me when she said, "Okefenokee Joe, you just don't understand cats. Have you ever seen the disappointed look on the cat's face when the animal finally dies?[2]

Streak had learned that he could stay safe from his enemies, high in the trees, or using his naturally beautiful bobcat coat to blend in with his surroundings. To most eyes he could become invisible. But it took a pileated woodpecker to teach him one more lesson about trees. And this is how it happened.

The pileated woodpecker is a year around resident in the

Okefenokee Swamp. It is the largest of the woodpecker family. Like many woodpeckers, its flight pattern is an up and down motion. Its food consists of mostly insects. Its shrill, almost comical call, can be heard a half a mile or more away, and its drumming or pecking on a hollow tree like the bellowing of an alligator, sounds like distant thunder echoing through the swamp. That's what it sounds like to me.

That bird is constantly carrying on and laughing outlandishly about something. It reminds me of that famous cartoon character Woody Woodpecker, invented by Walter Lanz. I am quite sure that Walter conceived the idea for Woody from the antics of the pileated woodpecker. I often see it and hear it pecking for insects.

I noticed Streak gazing up at it, just like I was. Then Streak looked at me, and I quickly said, "Go for it!" Streak immediately started up after the woodpecker. I saw right away the mistake my little friend was making, but unfortunately I had no way of warning him. I knew he would not understand me!

The woodpecker too, must have realized Streak's error because it casually looked down at Streak for a moment, and calmly turned back to its foraging. Every now and then it would tilt its head and watch Streak climbing up the tree. Still seemingly unconcerned, it would unhurriedly go back to searching for a meal under the bark of the tree.

One of his pecks loosened a large piece of bark, and it fell to the ground. Streak saw it, and slid down off the tree to investigate it. He pawed at it, and sniffed at it, and decided to go back up the tree after the woodpecker. He would sometimes stop climbing, and look up at the woodpecker. He had still not realized what he was doing wrong.

When Streak reached the same level as the woodpecker, it became obvious that suddenly he had finally realized his mistake. He had climbed at least one hundred feet up, and he was in the wrong tree! The woodpecker was eye to eye with him, but in a different tree, a full ten feet away!

The Pileated took one last look at streak, and flew away. His hilarious laughing song could be heard long after he had disappeared over the tree tops, and far back into the swamp. Streak had learned another very important lesson. But after he had come back down from the wrong tree, I didn't laugh or scold him for his error. We just continued our walk about. I am sure he learned what not to do next time, and he did not need any parental advice from me.

What I had seen though, convinced me all the more that wild animals must learn certain things through experience, and again Streak was no exception to the rule. Streak was growing wiser. He was also growing up, and growing older.

Notes:

[1] When a snake is frightened it will emit a foul smelling liquid substance from its two musk glands located on either side of its anus, toward its tail. Streak was rubbing that musk into the fur on his back. I believe wild animals do that to cover their own scent, so their prey or their enemies find it difficult to detct their presence.

[2] Sadly enough, to my knowledge the members of the cat family are the only wild animals that play with or torture their prey. All other carnivores make a quick kill. There is little or no suffering for the prey. Except for the cat family intentional cruelty does not exhist in the wild animal kingdom. I am often amazed, and sometimes dismayed by the distorted and unfair views and ideas about animals that some people exhibit.

Part 8: Squirrels Teach Lessons Too!

One day, on a walk about, we spotted two gray squirrels playing tag. They were chattering happily running up and down the trunk of a young cypress tree that stood near a small wooden bridge over a canal. The dark, tea colored, water under the bridge was about three feet deep.

By now, Streak had made a habit of looking up at me, waiting for me to give him the go ahead. Curious to see what he would do, I whispered, "Go for it!" And he did!

He made a dash for the cypress sapling! Both of the squirrels must have seen or sensed him coming, because before Streak was even close, they jumped to the railing on the left side of the bridge, about five feet away

Streak had reached the sapling, and as he was clutching its bark where the squirrels had been he saw that they had jumped over to the railing of the bridge! Without hesitation he easily jumped the five feet from the tree and landed on the railing, just as the squirrels had done. But again, the squirrels, realizing that a now terribly frenzied and determined bobcat was after them, decided to jump to the railing on the other side of the bridge, which was about eight feet away.

As my excited little friend reached that first railing, he saw the squirrels land on the other one. What happened next was one of the most comical, yet seriously unforgettable scenes I ever saw involving my tiny friend Streak! Yet, I had to force myself not to laugh.

The squirrels, perched on the far railing apparently thought that they were safe now, and they began to play tag again, chattering playfully back and forth at each other. I guess they didn't think that Streak could make that eight foot jump. But they were wrong!

Determined to catch at least one of the squirrels, Streak made a jump for that railing on the far side where the two squirrels were. He was in mid-air when the squirrels, both now chattering excitedly, leaped to the safety of another nearby tree on the far side of the bridge.

Streak made it to the railing alright, but he sailed right over it, and landed in the tea colored water of the canal below! Poor little kitten had miscalculated the distance. He made the eight foot jump alright, but he had missed the railing completely![1]

Thank goodness, the only living things that witnessed the whole scenario were the two squirrels and me. It was very difficult for me not to laugh, especially when he came out of the water he was soaking wet, and looking like a drowned rat. But I controlled myself as best I could.

So Streak learned that day that he must judge distances correctly. And two Grey Squirrels had taught him that.

His experience with those gray squirrels inadvertently had taught him another very valuable and important lesson. Streak had learned how to swim! And who says cats can't swim?[2]

Note:

[1] Many hunters, especially out in the West have often seen adult Panthers jump to catch their prey, and miss. They say that cats miss their intended prey more often than they catch it. That puts the odds in favor for the natural balance of nature.

[2] On our walk abouts, on hot days Streak would often crawl into a ditch, and soak in the water for a time. Obviously some cats are not adverse to water.

Part 9: Back into the Forest

It was now near the end of May. The bobcat mating season in South Georgia was in full swing. Streak the bobcat had been with me for a little more than three months. And what an adventure it had been for both of us. As Streak was learning how to be a real bobcat, I was learning from Streak about bobcats.

Along with Streak, under my care, I had twenty-five native snakes, thirteen American alligators, eleven Virginia whitetail deer, six raccoon's, four American black bears, two American river otters, two alligator snapping turtles, and several common snapping turtles, armadillos, and striped skunks.

And I'll say, for the rest of my life, that aside from caring for them, the most important thing I did with the animals under my care was to learn from them.

Streak was extra special because he had come to me as

a young kitten, and I had been given the golden opportunity to witness, at first hand, most of his early learning experiences. It had been quite an education for me, and I had come to dearly love my little companion.

Unbeknownst to the powers that be at the Park, for about a week now I had been leaving Streak's door open at night, and sometimes during the day. He was often free to come and go as he pleased. Although I knew I would really miss him, I was preparing him for his journey. The journey and the job, like all wild animals, he had been created to do for *God* and our *Blessed Mother Earth*.[1]

Of the many lessons I had learned from Streak, one of the most important was the fact that, as mentioned several times in this writing, although wild animals are born with inherent survival instincts, there are many skills they must learn by experience. They must also practice these skills

How to successfully calculate and jump certain distances, how to climb up and down a tree, how to pick the right tree to climb up after his prey, even how to sleep safely in the crotch of a branch high up in a tree. These were just a few of the experiential lessons that I witnessed while Streak was in his learning process.

He had learned to stalk and capture his prey. He had done that on his own. For that he had needed no help from me.

He had made many mistakes as a youngster, but now he was well prepared "to go it" on his own. Just like me he had now become swampwise.

In those few wonderful and rewarding months that Streak was by my side, I witnessed him practicing over and over again, the many skills a wild bobcat must master, in order to survive on its own. I can only suppose that had his momma been with him, he might have mastered all these things much earlier. But all he had was me.

I had been telling him over and over again, "All around us, for seven hundred and fifty square miles, is the great Okefenokee Swamp. You are a wild animal, Streak. The swamp belongs to you, and you belong to it. Anytime you want to go out there and be a real honest to *God* wild bob cat, you are free to do so."

On the afternoon of the twenty eighth of May, 1976, I was in my office on the phone. The door had been left open, and Streak walked in. Purring like a kitten, he jumped up on my shoulder. He placed his front paws over my right shoulder, his tummy on my shoulder, and his two rear legs on my chest. He clung there like that, hugging me. He stayed that way for quite a while. I said goodbye to the party on the other end of the line, and hung up the phone. When I tried to pull Streak off my shoulder, he insisted on remaining there. Finally, after about fifteen minutes had gone by, he let go.

He stayed close by me all that afternoon, until feeding time, when I said the magic words, "Chop, chop!" and he immediately did what he had become accustomed to doing when he heard that phrase. He ran into his enclosure eager to receive his meal.

As usual, I closed his door to feed him, and slid his favorite meal under the door to him. It was a whole turkey leg, raw warm, and fresh, just as he liked it.

At quitting time, just before I left the park for the day, I opened the door to the enclosure in which he had been living for the past three months, and as usual I said to my little friend, "See you later"!

I never saw Streak again.

Note:

[1] All living things on earth have been designed perfectly, by the Creator, to do the job that they have been created to do. All life in the natural world is necessary to the balance of the planet we humans live upon. Not one form of life is more important than the other. Because it is the combined effort of all living things, working at the job they have been created to do, that keeps the earth as it is, thus providing we humans an earth that we can live upon. Without the accomplishments provided by the constant teamwork of the natural world, we humans could not survive on this planet. This subject is considered at great length in another chapter in this writing.

CHAPTER 6
RIGHT BETWEEN THE EYES

Part 1: Enlightening Thoughts

My job in that swamp was a kid's dream come true. All I had to do was take care of the captive animals on exhibit at the park. I was supposed to feed them, keep them clean, make sure they had plenty of fresh water, and talk to the visitors about them. And I was loving it!

I was learning many wonderful and exciting things about bears, alligators, birds, rattlesnakes, and any and all of the local native wild creatures living in the swamp. I was getting my information first hand from the animals themselves. But the truth is, I was learning more from them than I was learning about them.

Believe it or not, although they were merely animals with tiny wild animal brains, collectively they were enlightening me with some surprising character lessons in teamwork, tolerance, patience, responsibility, forgiveness, and many other aspects akin to human nature, and behavior.

The most unique fact about what they were teaching me is that they could not read books to tell them what to do or how to act. They did it naturally, and the only sound explanation that truly made sense to me, is that they were, without question, simply following their creator's orders.[1]

Under my care at the park were thirteen huge American

alligators, and several smaller ones. I kept twelve native species of snakes on exhibit. I was also responsible for eleven Virginia whitetail deer, four American black bears, two American river otters, and an assortment of other small creatures. All of them were native to the area.

With such wondrous scenes of life, and matchless beauty all around me, coupled with my now close association with wild animals I had begun feeling in close harmony with the earth itself! I felt as if I was melting right into the scheme of things, and I found myself willingly, and happily becoming a part of it. Every aspect of my life was changing. I was beginning to see things, hear things, and think things that I had never thought about before in my entire life! I was truly becoming "Swampwise"!

For example, our scientific community recognizes over one million species and subspecies of insects sharing this earth with us. The entomologists say there are probably a million more that we do not yet know about! The most learned people on earth are still learning, and discovering new truths about the earth, and the life upon it!

Today, archeologists are still digging up bones, and finding the thrill of uncovering new and factual evidence, giving us more details about human history, and life on earth!

We refer to a medical doctor's work as "his practice". That is exactly what it is! Even the most learned medical doctor is still learning of, and how to treat sickness in the human body!

Astronomers study the stars, and the heavens. The ocean, and the life in it, is being studied by marine biologists. The human race is still in the learning stages about planet earth, the galaxy, and virtually anything, and everything! We are still learning!

In the Okefenokee Swamp it suddenly hit me right between the eyes that the mere fact that we humans do not know, and are still trying to learn, should be a constant reminder, and humble all people of all lands to the fact, that we humans did none of the creating!

It was all here! Everything, including the planets, the atmosphere, and its systems, all the plant and animal life, even the earth itself, everything had been created before mankind appeared. We did not "invent" any of it! It was all, every bit of it, here before we got here!

The *Holy Bible* tells us all about that in the book of *Genesis*. In so many words it states that the human race was the last form of life on earth to be created. Believe it or not, modern day science completely backs up what the *Bible* says on that subject! And here is why!

A moment ago we were discussing insects. We are able to identify each species of insect simply by the way it is built. Imagine that! Trillions upon trillions of tiny bodies of all different shapes and sizes are performing minute tasks everywhere on earth, and all at the same time! Coupled with the work of the plant, and animal life, the combined effort of all, results in a beautiful, environmentally healthy planet earth, fit for humans to live upon. We humans simply could not exist on the earth, if it were not suitable habitat for us!

Not fully realizing most of those facts, a lot of us think of insects only as useless and lower forms of life. And we do not like them! We see an insect, we squash it! They irritate us, and we squash them because we are bigger than they are, and we can do it!

Yet, all those pesky, seemingly-useless, insignificant, and unwanted insects are actually essential team members of *God's Creation*! All of them are working constantly for the earth! Should they all die or disappear, should those many minute tasks cease to be performed, in no time at all life on this planet would change so drastically, that we humans could probably not live here either! Without those "pesky" insects man could possibly not exist on this planet! And that is serious!

That same exact thing would happen if all the trees were gone! Why the environment has become a political issue in our country is beyond my comprehension. It should concern everyone on this earth! But because it is a political issue, and a current one, more people are aware of the fact that plants, including trees, help keep the atmosphere clean by producing much needed oxygen, and consuming nitrogen. It's a well-known and established scientific fact that without trees we humans could not survive here on this planet! Although it is not a well-known fact, the same thing would probably happen if all the insects were gone!

On the other hand, it dawned on me that the entire human race could vanish from the face of the earth, and there is not an insect or a tree in the forest that would miss us!

Nature does not need man! Nature is perfect! Why should it not be? It has all been created by *God*! Probably, if nature had her way, she would spit us out because of how we so ignorantly mistreat it! No, nature does not need man!

But man needs nature! Man could not exist on this planet without nature, and the works of nature!

And that is where science agrees with the book of *Genesis* in *the Holy Bible!* In the very beginning, before the earth could become suitable habitat for humans, it was absolutely necessary that all forms of life and all things in the natural world become established here first! Otherwise, we could not exist here! And the *Bible* tells us that is exactly what *God* did in the first five days.

Such were the deep thoughts and understandings that were coming into my mind night and day in the Okefenokee Swamp! The door of understanding was opening wide for me, and new thoughts and realizations were constantly hitting me right between the eyes!

Note:

[1] All living things on earth have been designed perfectly, by the Creator, to do the job that they have been created to do. All life in the natural world is necessary to the balance of the planet we humans live upon. Not one form of life is more important than the other. Because it is the combined effort of all living things, working at the job they have been created to do, that keeps the earth as it is, thus providing we humans an earth that we can live upon. Without the accomplishments provided by the constant teamwork of the natural world, we humans could not survive on this planet. This subject is considered at great length in another chapter in this writing.

"Swampwise"

Part 2: The Stranger in the Swamp

One evening, just before dark, I was relaxing on the steps of my front porch with a cup of coffee in my hand, watching the swift dragon flies as they zoomed through the air catching wary mosquitoes. At the same time insects of all sorts were busy working at their jobs on the ground all around me. A gray squirrel was on a branch of the big live oak tree, munching on one last hickory nut, before retiring. I could hear the pieces of its shell hitting the ground under the tree.

I saw the flashing glow of an early summer firefly over by the woodpile. The crickets and the frogs were beginning to sing their nightly chorus. Off in the distance I could hear the faint sound of a Chuckwill's Widow tuning up for his nightly songs. The little brown bats were leaving their daytime quarters and darting around in the early darkness. Already they were acting as the night time crew, taking over for the dragon flies, as they too were after the mosquitoes. The red winged black birds were talking quietly to each other, as they picked out roosting spots for the night.

I could not help but feel amazed at the wondrous beauty of the busy and teeming life all around me. I felt so thankful to *God* for placing me where I was on this earth! Suddenly it dawned upon me that all my life, up until now, how thoughtlessly and unconcernedly I had taken nature, and scenes such as I was seeing right then, for granted.

How wrong I was to have always just assumed that birds should be beautiful, and sing pretty songs. Dragon flies were just supposed to be out there flying around catching mosquitoes. Ants and roaches were made to crawl around on the ground. Frogs and crickets were meant to sing at night.

I had always felt that it's only natural that bats were blind, or that they should fly at night, and birds should be active during the day. Deer are naturally timid, graceful, and able to run fast. I expected the sun to come up in the east in the morning and set in the west at night.

I had never fully realized until that moment just how well

planned and how perfectly executed *God's* plan for life on earth really is!

Centuries ago He had designed such a complete fantastic and intricate system of checks and balances all across the earth, that probably no one human being could ever possibly comprehend it all.

Along with that thought it dawned on me that all the life around me in that swamp had been there for thousands of generations before I had arrived, and it would be there long after I was gone. I had nothing to do with creating it, and there was no way I could improve upon it.

I was the only living thing in the swamp that was not a part of the plan, and the realization suddenly hit me right between the eyes that I was the only stranger in the Okefenokee Swamp! I was the only thing in that swamp that was not necessary!

I was now at the threshold of becoming truly "Swampwise!" From that moment on my life had changed forever!

Part 3: Teamwork

Another of the many observations and lessons that hit me right between the eyes is concerned with teamwork. I was eagerly discovering that in all facets of life on earth, cooperation and teamwork was involved! No one member of the team is more important than the other, because it's the team effort of all, working together, that makes it work. Nothing works without teamwork!

Just about every play in a football game is designed to make a touchdown. The success of the play depends upon the efforts each and every member of the team. If one player fails to do his part, or doesn't make the right block, the play fails.

Every part of an automobile engine is part of the team that makes the engine work properly. One part fails, the engine fails.

Every part of the human body is part of the team that keeps

the body going. If one part fails, the body can no longer function properly. Without teamwork, nothing works!

The same exact principle applies to the intricate workings of all of *God's Creation* in the natural world. All things living or nonliving, are equal in their importance, because all things in the natural world, are solid members of nature's team!

Ants are no more important than grasshoppers, bears are no more important than deer. A rock or a tree is no more important than a blade of grass, or a babbling brook. Lightning is no more important than the sun or the rain. Because it is the team effort of all things in the natural world working together that makes it work. And nothing works without teamwork!

Every insect or plant, and every wild animal has been placed on this earth with definite responsibilities. Each one has its own job to perform. The major concern of all forms of life in the natural world is helping to maintain the balance of life on the earth.

It's common knowledge that every blade of grass and every leaf on every plant or tree helps to purify the atmosphere and create oxygen. As part of nature's team, the plants of *God's* earth do much more than that. During the entire life of a plant it will provide food and shelter for countless other living things. Some of which we cannot see with the naked eye. And when a plant dies, it will naturally recycle back into the earth and become food for other living things. Nothing in the natural world is ever allowed to go to waste!

Ever since the beginning, plants have provided most, if not all of the necessities of mankind. They add beauty to the earth by providing countless memorable scenes of beautiful, truly amazing landscapes. Plants feed us, and clothe us. They give us tools, shelter, and medicine. And almost every book we read was once a tree!

Wild animals in many ways also demonstrate how nature allows nothing to go to waste! For example everything the American black bear does out there in the woods is helping to maintain the balance of the earth. Every time it runs down a deer, which it certainly can do, it catches the weak one, the sick one, the slow one. It helps to keep the herd strong and healthy. Every time it tears up a palmetto bush to get its delicious bud, it crops the plant and helps it to grow better the following year! Every time it defecates, it fertilizes the land, and it plants seeds. And when a bear dies, just like when a blade of grass dies, it will naturally recycle back into the earth and become food for other life and in other ways. Nothing goes to waste.

Another aspect of the job that wild animals were created to do is the fact that they only go where they are needed. If there is a job that needs being done anywhere on earth to maintain or correct the balance, sooner or later the right animal will be there on the job to correct it!

In my lectures I often pointed out that, "If you are like most people, and you don't want snakes in your yard, one thing you can try to do is get rid of what brought the snake there. If there are no more rats and mice, you won't see snakes in your yard either!"

Snakes don't just happen to appear in people's yards. They have been called there to do a job. A part of the job the snake has been created to do is to help control the number of rodents in any given area.

The more I was given to understand, the more fascinated I became with the workings of such a complete, and amazing master plan for the earth, that *God* had created so many centuries ago!

With this book I have done my best to relate and share my "Swampwise" experiences, and the importance of what I learned from them. I am doing this because just like the plants and animals, I feel that I am merely "following orders!"

CHAPTER 7

THE AMERICAN BLACK BEAR

Part 1: Getting to Know the Bears

At one time I had four American black bears under my care. I was with those bears twenty four hours a day when I wanted to. And back then I wanted to twenty four hours a day. I was learning a lot of interesting facts about bears. But more importantly, the bears were teaching me, and helping me to understand countless exciting and valuable swampwise facts about all the life in the natural world around me.[1]

I'll never forget Black Jack. That bear grew to be six hundred and fifty pounds, and he was healthy. He wasn't a world record, but for an American black bear he was big! When he stood up on his hind legs I could not reach up and touch the top of his head. He was that tall! Black Jack was an excellent example of an American black bear for our exhibit.

The bears were on display in a natural habitat compound at the park. They could be seen safely through a large picture glass window in the lobby of the Serpentarium. Since bears have a tendency not to put up with the presence of another bear, I kept no more than two on exhibit at a time. Usually that would be one male and one female.[2]

Once a day, in the evening, I fed my bears a mixture of dry dog food mixed with honey. That was their main diet, and they loved it.

They also received an assortment of fruits and vegetables. They loved that too. Bears just love to eat.[3]

Sometimes I would go out into the compound with a bucket of 'goodies' for the bears, and call Black Jack up. He knew he was about to get a treat! I would see that huge black bear rise up out of the green palmettos, stand up on its hind legs, and come running straight towards me like a freight train! He'd always stop right in front of me, and sit down. Thank goodness he didn't sit on me! He was really, really big![4]

The first thing he would do was to put his paws down to his side, as if to show me he meant me no harm. He had claws four inches long! They were not sharp like cat claws, but even a friendly love tap from that big and mighty bear could have possibly knocked my head off!

He would sit there like a big puppy dog. I'd scratch his ears for a while. He seemed to enjoy that. Then I would reach into the bucket, and pull out a tiny grape, and hand it to him. That big black bear would always take that delicious little morsel from my fingers with his tongue. He would never use his teeth or his claws on me. He would not intentionally hurt me. But that was because by now he knew me. I was not a stranger to him. No one I know, including myself, could do all that with a wild black bear and get away with it. If a person ever tried to scratch wild bear's ears, the bear would most certainly tear that fool to pieces!

Black Jack taught me a lot about bears. One day, during the time that he was still housed in an iron barred cage, I noticed him watching me a little closer than usual. I was cleaning out his water pan at the time. Curious to see what he had in mind, I turned off the hose, and asked him, "Hey Black Jack what's up?"

Of course, he did not answer me. He looked up at the heavy chain link fencing that stretched across the top of his iron barred cage. No longer looking at me, he stood up on his hind legs, reached up and took hold of the chain link fence with his claws. Then he turned his head in my direction, and I could see him looking at me again, out of the corner of his eye. He seemed to be making sure I was watching him. And I was watching him, very intently! He then grabbed a two inch link of the fence with his teeth, and still watching me, with his powerful jaws he squeezed it until it bent it all the way down to one inch. I stood there amazed at that feat! That bear was strong! It was like, by that action, he was saying to me, "Chief, I can get out of here any time I want to."

I never saw him do that again.

To my knowledge he never even tried to escape. He had been captive raised from a tiny cub, and had no idea what freedom in the wilderness was all about. He was content with his life as it was. I have often wondered, "Why in the world did he show me that trick?"

I guess I will never know.

Hugh was the name of another male bear under my care. He weighed a little less than four hundred pounds. When Hugh was tiny his teeth and his claws had been removed. Obviously, whoever had him in their possession was planning to make a pet of him.

Humans should know better than to think of any wild animal as their 'house pet'. Wild animals might make interesting pets, but they do not make good pets. Most people want a pet that will come to them when they call it, or one that will do as they say, and obey various demanding commands, one that will show them love, and gratitude.

A true wild animal is born to be self-reliant and self-sufficient. The way *God* intended it to be. It will never, under any circumstances, recognize a human as its master. A good animal trainer can teach it to perform for an audience, but it is not the trainer's pet. And virtually all of the "teaching" is done by taking advantage of the animal's instinctive desire for food. The deal is service and reward. You do this trick for me, and I will reward you with this food!

Hugh had no way to defend himself, and could never be released into the wild. He was doomed to stay in captivity all of his life. I really don't think he minded that tho, because, just like Black Jack, he had been captured at an early age, and he had not yet had time to learn the joys or the hardships of freedom. At least his existence was serving an educational purpose. Throughout his lifetime his four hundred pounds of black bear were seen, and photographed by thousands of thrilled and happy spectators! All things considered, without claws and teeth, he was better off where he was.

Another bear under my care had been given the name of June. She was a two hundred and fifty pound female. She was unfriendly, and very unpredictable. Sometimes when I approached her cage to feed her or check on her, she would make the "yeng, yeng, yeng" sound that black bears make when they are upset, or uptight about something. She would slam her body against the bars, trying to frighten me away! Whoever had her before the game commission confiscated her and gave her to us must have really maltreated her. My guess was that already she was much too old and set in her ways to be friendly, and tolerate me. I knew that unlike Black Jack, if I were to try and scratch her ears, she would tear my arm off! I treated her as fairly and gently as I did all the bears, but I never tried to make friends with her.

Betsy was another small female American black bear under my care. She weighed right at two hundred pounds. She was a lot more gentle and easy going than June, but I learned I could not really trust her either. One day as I was cleaning her cage she was acting friendly and calm, and I decided to see if she would let me scratch her ears like I had done with Black Jack many a time. I took the chance, and I slid my arms through her iron barred cage, reaching for her ears.

Immediately her attitutude abruptly changed. The almost friendly cooing sound she had been making turned to an outright cry of shock and fear. Her ears were bent back, and the hair on her head and shoulders was bristling. I could tell she wanted no part of me touching her. So I quickly backed off, and away from her!

I saw no need to ever try that again! Adult Black Bears do not need human affection. Not a bit! Truth be known no wild animal does!

"Swampwise"

Notes:

[1] I have often said that, "The Okefenokee Swamp was my textbook, and experience my teacher."

[2] Bears are solo animals. Unlike wolves or coyotes, they do not travel in packs. Sometimes, if a fishing hole is exceptionally good, they might congregate around it. But usually the only time they are seen together is during the mating season. Or nowadays at garbage dump!

[3] Each Monday I would drive the park truck into town to pick up supplies. I had made a deal with several grocery stores that I could have the fresh foods they were unable to sell over the weekend. I would get all sorts of meats, vegetables, and fruits for the bears, deer, and other furry creatures, and fish for the alligators.

[4] When a bear stands up on its hind legs, and begins to walk around, it looks as if it is awkward, and clumsy. Don't be fooled. A bear is extremely agile, and like a football player, no matter how fast it is running, it can turn or stop on dime!

Part 2: Mating Season

At one time, we had little June on exhibit along with Black Jack in the natural habitat bear compound. The two of them had gotten used to the presence of each other, and they seemed to be getting along just fine. They just never got close to each other. Until the day little June came in heat.

She began to nervously walk around the compound uttering a clucking sound which could easily be interpreted as a desire to find a mate. Almost immediately Black Jack became aware of her situation, and he was hot on her trail. Little June was not even half the size of Black jack, and even in heat, she was acting as if she was afraid of him. He would follow her, intentionally staying at least ten feet behind her. He would paw at the ground at her foot prints, and lift his paw up to his nose and sniff it. And he would make that unmistakable "glugh, glugh" bear sound that means it wants something. It became obvious that they both wanted to mate, but neither one was exactly sure how to go about it.

Curiously enough, sometimes while Black Jack was sniffing his paws with the scent of June on them, he would look over at me, making his "I want something" sound, as if he was asking,

"What am I supposed to do, Chief? Can you help me?"

To my knowledge, neither Black Jack nor June had ever been with another bear before, and it is certain that neither one had ever mated. I was wishing I could help them, but they were bears, and they would have to figure things out by themselves.

A day went by. Black Jack, in his eagerness, had been trying to mount June. But even though she was in the middle of heat and needing him, she still seemed to be afraid of him, and acted as if she wanted nothing to do with him. If he approached her, she would slap at him fiercely with the claws of her front paws, giving out with that, "yeng, yeng, yeng" sound of intimidation bears make, when they feel confused or uncertain.

I did not get to see them mate, and I wasn't sure that they had. But several days later June seemed to have taken on a new and different attitude. That fierce little bear began to act what I called almost cuddly. She actually seemed friendly and gentle. I suppose part of that impression was caused by the whimpering almost childlike sounds she had begun to make.

A wild female black bear will pick out a safe place to bear her young long before she becomes pregnant. And after mating with a male bear, when it comes time she will go there, and stay there quietly, until her young are born. This is usually during the winter months in South Georgia.

After a few days of watching her, I decided that she had definitely mated with Black Jack, and she was pregnant! Knowing that she now needed a safe haven, I scattered a bale of straw in her holding pen, filled up her heavy metal water container, and put some food down for her. Her favorite treat was a vanilla ice cream cone. So with a vanilla ice cream cone, I coaxed her back into her enclosure.

In the next several weeks and months she began to look and

act so pregnant. I'd hear her moaning and whimpering. When I'd go out there to look in on her she didn't rush at the bars trying scare or hurt me, like she had always done before. No, she'd just lie there, acting like a pregnant bear should act, and looking up at me as if to say, "I'm going to be a momma!"

When, after a few months, she began to get heavier by the day, it was obvious that she wasn't faking her pregnancy!

As winter approached, and the time was near for her to deliver, I began to check on her more often. Because black bears in captivity have been known to eat or kill their young, my plan was to steal the cubs from her, before she could do any harm to them.

But I could not be with her twenty four hours a day, and as luck would have it, I missed my opportunity to save the cubs by a mile! I walked out there one morning, and I found her lying next to a bloody mess. She had delivered two tiny cubs, a male and a female, during the night, and had murdered them both! She had taken the terrible deed one step further by devouring a part of each of them!

Disgusted and disappointed, I sadly removed what was left of the two offspring and most of the straw from her holding pen. And as I was doing so, she began slamming her body against the bars again, trying to frighten me away, just as she had always done before her pregnancy began. It was disappointing, but things with the bears were now back to normal.

Part 3: Moving the Bears

For years at the Okefenokee Swamp Park, all of the American black bears were on exhibit separately in small iron barred cages. Each cage was about twenty by twenty feet square. Most of the time, through boredom, the bears would pace back and forth in those small lonely enclosures. The powers that be finally decided to build a natural habitat compound for them. That way the bears might be a little healthier and happier. And by viewing them safely through a huge picture glass window, the public could see them up close in their natural habitat!

We partially cleared a large area in back of the Serpentarium, and surrounded it with a ten-foot high chain link fence, topped with two strands of barbed wire. To insure that our visitors could always see the bears, we put up an electrified fence inside the compound. There were five strands of barbed wire in that fence, and it was disguised, so that our viewers could not see it. Its purpose was to keep the bears in view at all times.

The time came to bring the bears out of their iron barred cages, and place them on exhibit in their new quarters. Our bears had always been housed in separate cages. They had never been together. And since bears in the wild are not known to hang out together, I convinced the management that it would be wise to put one bear in at a time. Before we added another one, we should make sure that the first one had become accustomed to its surroundings. That's what we did, and Black Jack was the first in line for the job!

With a honey coated biscuit, I coaxed Black Jack out of his cage, and into a bear trap on wheels, that we had borrowed from the State Game Commission. Before I put him in the compound, out of curiosity, I drove up town to the truck stop, and weighed him. Black Jack weighed six hundred and fifty pounds. He was big and he was healthy, and a prime example of the American black bear for our exhibit.

Wondering what would happen when Black Jack touched the electric fence was my main concern about this project. Would he panic? Would he burst through it? What would his reaction be?

When I turned him loose in the compound, he did what most bears would do. He began to investigate his new surroundings. He checked out the big hollow oak tree that would be his shelter. With a huge front paw he tested the water in the cement pool we had built for him. He sniffed and pawed at things at random, and he rubbed his back on a tall slash pine tree. Finally he found the electric fence.

"Swampwise"

The shock took him totally by surprise. Since bears have poor eyesight he probably had not even seen it. He made that "yeng, yeng yeng" sound that bears make when they are in pain or panic, and jumped back! Then he did something I never would have thought he would do. He crashed his way right through that fence and disappeared into the foliage beyond it. In a hair of a second, he was out of sight! He was still fenced in within the compound, but because of the dense foliage he could not be seen from the viewing area!

This would never do! If management found out about it, they would have my head! So, for the moment, I did not tell them. I knew I must do something, and do it quickly! But I also knew that Black Jack would be extremely hesitant to come back through that electric fence, and 'quickly' might be all but impossible!

Right away I began to remove that electric fence. It took me two hours. Black Jack stayed way in the back. I really felt sorry for him, because I knew that he was still confused and frightened, by something he couldn't possibly understand!

With the fence gone, I began calling to him. I had some honey buns in my hand, and I rubbed some of their sweet icing onto the trees and some of the bushes. I knew that, along with its eyesight, the bear's sense of smell is also poor. But I was hoping that if I scattered the smell of the honey buns in enough places, he'd get a whiff of them, and maybe come to me.

After about an hour I heard him slowly and cautiously coming toward me. The honey buns were doing their job. As he came closer, I backed up towards the open door of the bear trap. He followed me all the way to the trap, and making sure he saw me, I quickly threw the honey buns into it! Black Jack went straight in after them, and I closed the door. Once again, problem solved, except for one thing: How were we going to keep the bears in view so our visitors could see them?

The only answer that made sense was to put the electric fence back up, but this time use heavier gauge wire, and increase the voltage. That is what we did, and to make sure Black Jack would see it, this time I tied pieces of bright colored cloth to it. Hopefully, the dangling cloth would warn him of the presence of the wire. That being done, we released Black Jack into the compound again.

Once more he went about investigating his surroundings. When he finally came to the electric wire, he hesitated. It could be that he had seen the bright cloth hanging from it, or possibly he had seen the wire. He might even have smelled it. Whatever the reason he backed away from it.

In a short while, after he had gone around checking other things, he came back to the wire. He sniffed at it curiously before touching it with his paw. Obviously it gave him quite a shock, because he jumped back, giving out with a loud "yeng, yeng, yeng" sound! And in a frantic attempt to get as far away from it as he could, he ran to the far side of the compound. He stayed there whimpering, and making that same sound of utter fear and confusion he had made before, upon touching the other wire.

It took a long time for Black Jack to calm down, and begin to walk around in his surroundings again. But I noticed that he would not go near that wire.

We watched Black Jack closely for about a week, allowing him to become accustomed to his new home. He approached the electric fence many times, but to my knowledge he never again got near enough to touch it. It seemed to me that maybe he was just periodically checking to see if the wire was still there.

We put little June in there with Black Jack, and it took a while, but they both did become acclimated to being together in their new habitat. Our visitors were thrilled to be able to safely observe black bears in such close proximity![1]

Note:

[1] Little June's first reaction to her new surroundings in the bear compound is described in detail elsewhere in this writing.

Part 4: Bears Can't Help It!

Bears love honey. They can't help it. Wild bears have been known to become so excited over honey, that while they are tearing into a bee hive to get at it, they'll even eat the bees, and parts of the hive! It's just a natural and well-known fact that bears love honey.

Each year the bee keepers in South Georgia put out a great many honey bee hives in and around the Okefenokee Swamp. Their living depends on those hives to produce quality honey for the market.

Just as natural as bears love honey, the bee keepers are constantly at war with the bears. No matter how the keepers try to protect their hives from the bears, the bears will figure out a way to get to them. And most of the time they don't just get the honey, they destroy the entire hive!

Bright lights, fences, or loud noises do not deter them. If the fence is electric the bear will just dig under it, or bravely crash right through it! The bee keepers have learned that the only sure way to keep bears out of their apiaries is to shoot them!

The Georgia State Game Commission had become concerned about what this problem was doing to the bear population in Georgia. One day an officer from the Game Commission visited me at the park. It seems that the state had a plan to stop bears from raiding apiaries! To me, the plan sounded humane for the bears, and it just might solve the dilemma of the bee keepers. It was a good plan, and if it worked, it might save a few bears, financial disasters for the bee keepers, and a lot of shotgun shells!

It seems that out in Oklahoma the ranchers were having the same serious problem as the beekeepers in Georgia. But with coyotes, not bears, and with chicken houses, not bee hives. The coyotes were breaking into the chicken houses at night, and killing scores of chickens on each raid. The ranchers were losing a great deal of their income because of this, and they were up in arms about it.[1]

So their State Game Commission was forced to come up with a possible solution. They did, and it worked! For them!

It involved a chemical known as lithium chloride. It's a substance that has no odor and no taste. If taken internally it is not lethal, but it will cause a violent reaction in the stomach and all related digestive organs. Possibly the use of this chemical could teach coyotes to stay away from chickens.

So they laced several pounds of raw chicken meat and a few feathers with the substance. That night, after dark they placed some of it in several chicken houses. Before daylight they removed it. After a week or so the night time raids ceased! The plan had actually worked! The coyotes in that vicinity had been taught to avoid chickens. The method was introduced to every chicken farmer in Oklahoma. And soon the coyotes across Oklahoma stopped raiding chicken houses.[2]

Upon becoming aware of those results with coyotes in Oklahoma, the Georgia State Game Commission decided to experiment, using lithium chloride, with the black bears of South Georgia.

They were interested in the bears under my care. Of course the park would be honored to take part in the experiment, and the Park's management happily granted the state permission to begin!

On a Saturday morning, a spoonful of honey, dosed with lithium chloride was given to the bears. Each one of them became violently ill.

In just a few minutes after swallowing it, little June vomited, and defecated all over herself, and her cage.

It took a little while, but Hugh also succumbed to his dose, and became ill with a violently upset stomach, just as June had done.

Betsy, our other small female, displayed much the same reaction as the others. For a while it looked as if Black Jack was having no ill effects from his dosage. But after about twenty minutes he too began to show the same ill effects as the other

"Swampwise"

bears had done. So apparently the chemical worked on all of the bears.

The unanimous conclusion was that just as with the coyotes, lithium chloride would definitely make bears sick. The next step in the experiment would be to see if bears would now refuse to eat honey.

The following Saturday the bears were offered pure honey with no additives. Some of the results were almost comical. If the experiment hadn't been so seriously important, we might have laughed.

June was first in line. Poor thing, the mere sight of that spoonful of pure honey sent her to the far side of her cage. She was afraid to even get near it! She was frantically making the "yeng, yeng, yeng" sound that bears make when they are deathly afraid of something! She definitely became ill, and began regurgitating. The mere sight and smell of honey made her do that!

Hugh did not even get close to his spoonful. He took one look at it, and vomited on the spot. Making a similar sound as that of June, in seemingly utter panic he turned his back on it, and leaped to the far end of his cage! He was crying, "Yeng yeng, yeng, aww, aww, aww" and would not even look at that spoon full of 'awful stuff!'

Betsy sniffed at her spoonful, made a few clucking sounds of desire, and for a moment she acted as if she was going to eat it. But suddenly, as if she remembered her last incident with honey, making the same sound as the others, she backed off. However, although she avoided the honey, she did not become ill, or regurgitate like the others. She just backed away, and stayed away.

So apparently the use of lithium chloride would work on bears. They would associate the mere sight or smell of honey with that terrible sickness they had experienced the last time they ate it! Because of that they would absolutely not even touch it. Maybe we had found the solution to the problem!

But now we had come to Black Jack, our biggest bear. He had

been hearing the sounds of the others, and because Betsy was in the cage next to him, he had seen her reaction to her spoonful of honey. Throughout the entire process of feeding honey to the other bears, he had been making that "glugh, glugh" sound, which, when translated means "I want some of that!"

He was making that sound when we offered him his spoonful of pure honey. He put his nose through the iron bars, and sniffed at it. Instantly he turned his nose up at it, and backed a few feet away from it. Then surprisingly enough, he calmly sat down. We were right in the middle of our lithium chloride experiment with him, and he just sat down! It was almost as if he was thinking things over.

He eventually got back up, and walked over to the spoon again. Black Jack was not making the clucking sound now. He sniffed at the spoon of honey, and once again he backed away, but this time he did not sit down. In an instant he turned back around and quickly took the honey, spoon and all, in his mouth. And to our dismay, he swallowed the honey! In one split second, our experiment had failed! Later he dropped the spoon.

Black Jack had been acting as if he were thinking to himself, "You know, last time I ate honey I got really sick, but that must have been just a bad batch. I love honey! I'm going to eat this! I don't care if I get sick or not!"

Because of one bear, our Black Jack, the experiment failed! It was concluded that lithium chloride would work on some bears, but not all bears. That being the case, the state of Georgia immediately dropped the idea, and the bee keepers, even today, are still at war with the American back bear, and they are still losing money, and wasting shotgun shells!

Months went by. Eventually all of the bears would get over their fear of honey, and return to eating it, and enjoying it. Hugh was the last bear to go back to it. I really felt sorry for him, because for months at the mere sight of honey he would toss his cookies, and try to hide in the corner of his cage, while uttering his "yeng, yeng, yeng", bear cry of distress. Finally, after a year even Hugh went back to eating honey. I guess "All is well that ends well!"

Notes:

[1] One of the rules of conduct for a wild animal is not to waste. And under natural conditions the rule is strictly obeyed. The one and only exception occurs when human practices change the game. All wild animals, including coyotes must be constantly vigilant, and for them it's a twenty four hour a day, seven days a week task just to survive, and just to find something to eat. They often go hungry for days on end. When they come across easy pickings like a huge house full of chickens, they can't help but get excited, and out of control! They never had it so good! The coyote will grab one chicken, and while it is taking a bite out of it, spot another chicken! It'll drop the first chicken, and go after the second one. Coyotes have been known to kill large numbers of chickens in one night. The same scenario is true when a raccoon comes across a farmer's corn field! Wow! That raccoon never had it so good!

[2] The consumption of raw chicken laced with lithium chloride made each coyote violently ill. For twenty four hours or more it was vomiting, and defecating almost constantly. The next time it smelled or saw a chicken, it associated it with that horrible sickness, and would not go near it!

CHAPTER 8

RESIDENT ALLIGATORS OF THE OKEFENOKEE

Part 1: The King

I had seen alligators all my life. I really didn't know much about them until I moved into the Great Okefenokee Swamp in Southeastern Georgia. For almost ten years, along with the bears, the bobcats, the snakes, the deer, and all the other wild creatures, they were my next door neighbors. Each and every one of those animals helped me to gain wisdom, and become swampwise! And I came to love and respect all of them, including the American alligator.

For me, it was a true blessing to have been given the wonderful opportunity to observe them at close hand, on a regular daily and at times, nightly basis. What a wealth of first hand experiential knowledge I gained from them, and about them.

Oscar was a big alligator. He was almost fourteen feet long. I used to joke about the fact that, no one knew how much he weighed, because no one ever picked him up! The truth is that no wild animal in the swamp would threaten or get near a bull gator that large. He was definitely "The King of the Okefenokee!" That's for sure!

He wasn't tame, and he was by no means a captive. He was a natural born wild alligator, and he had claimed the whole of the Okefenokee Swamp Park as his kingdom. Because he was not fenced in, he was free to roam anywhere in the swamp that struck his fancy.

Never did Oscar show any sign of animosity toward a human. He was a massive, powerfully strong, and potentially dangerous wild animal. Yet he consistently amazed everyone at the park, myself included, by his passive attitude, and behavior toward people.

A striking example of just how accommodating, and easy going Oscar really was around humans, was demonstrated every spring. The ditches and small canals in the main park area needed to be cleared of last year's dying vegetation and other debris. To accomplish this several employees would get into the water and pull most of it out by hand. At times we were in the water for hours. Every so often Oscar would be lying in the canal in a spot that needed cleaning out. As we'd get closer to him, he seemed to realize he was in the way, and he would casually move elsewhere. Had he been of the mind set to harm any of us, he was often given the opportunity to do so. But as big as he was, and as wild as he was, as long as he lived he never harmed a human.

The King passed away in 2005, but his memory lives on. This is a part of his story.[1]

There was one particular small island in the park that Oscar seemed to favor. We named it "Oscar's Island." It was in plain view of our visitors, and he spent a good deal of his time on it, basking in the sun. This arrangement made for excellent public relations for the park, because all of our visitors would be guaranteed to see a really big wild gator in its natural habitat! There were thousands of pictures taken of Oscar during his reign of fifty plus years at the park! In his prime, Oscar was almost as famous as the Governor of Georgia!

Several times during the day, for the enjoyment of our public, I would walk out into the main area of the park with a five gallon bucket containing a few fresh fish. As I walked over to where Oscar was, I would begin giving out with a few of my world famous Okefenokee Joe gator calls.[2]

This would attract any visitors within the sound of my voice.

As they gathered around me, I would tell them where they should stand to safely watch the show! Next I would reach into the five gallon bucket, pull out a fish, and wave it at Oscar! At my, "Hup, hup" command, he would stand up on all four legs and walk down off his island into the canal. That scene, in itself, was a thrilling sight for our already enthused audience! Then he would swim the short distance between us, and come up out of the water to me. As he did this, I would always hear the excited "oohs and ahhs" of the tourists. Most of them had never seen a real live alligator, let alone watch one move, and seem to obey commands, especially an alligator as big as Oscar! He would stop right in front of me and lie down. Holding a nice big fish by the tail, I would lightly tap him on his nose with it. He would open his mouth wide, and I'd toss the fish in! His jaws would slam shut, and my enraptured audience would watch him lift his head up, and swallow it usually in one great gulp![3]

A few moments later he would slip back into the water. That would be the end of our show, and the excited and satisfied crowd would then disburse.

One day, I had just finished a show with Oscar, and most of the spectators had moved on. As I was picking up my empty five gallon bucket, I noticed one elderly lady still standing there by the canal. She was gazing intently at Oscar. I heard her say his name several times. And just as she had seen me do with a fish, she began waving her purse at him. To my surprise Oscar turned and began to swim over to her. I thought to myself, "Uh Oh! Look out little lady!"

Obviously excited by Oscar's response, the lady quickly put her purse on the ground, and began rummaging through it, frantically looking for her camera! She was not watching Oscar, but I was! Oscar had come up out of the water, and was moving straight toward her! I dropped the fish bucket and ran over to her, shouting, "Watch out! Watch out!"

She was still fumbling with her purse, and still totally unaware of Oscar's approach. I quickly grabbed her by her arm and pulled her out of the way! But her purse was left there lying there, wide open, on the ground! From a safe distance, we watched Oscar. Without hesitating, he took the lady's purse in his mighty jaws, and lay down.

Thank God he did not swallow it like he had done earlier with the fish. He just held it in his mouth. We could see its brown leather strap dangling from one side of his mouth. When the lady fully realized what had just happened, and what the consequences might have been, she became terrified! I did my best to calm her down, and I told her not to worry because I would get her purse back for her. Of course, I had no idea how I would do that, but I had to say something to calm her down.

Oscar stayed right there for quite a while with the purse in his mouth. I was reasonably sure that by now he must have realized that it was not a fish and that whatever it was it was not fit to eat! But he kept it in his mouth.

After about ten minutes he got up and slid back into the water. The purse and all of its contents was still in his mouth. He did not swim away; he just stayed there close to the bank of the canal. It was as if he was still mulling it over as to what to do with that thing in his mouth.

Finally he made a decision. Unceremoniously he dropped it in the water, and left it behind. As we watched it slowly sinking to the bottom, Oscar was swimming back toward his island.

With my gator pole I fished the purse out of the water. Virtually everything in it, including the lady's camera was soaking wet. I handed it to the lady, she thanked me, and a short time later she and her husband left the park.[4]

Incidents like that seldom occurred in the park. Most people were cooperative with our rules. There were signs scattered around asking people not to feed, pet or tease the animals, especially the alligators. And as they entered the park, for safety's sake, they were instructed to stay on the cement walkways. Every now and then some clown would show up and try all manner of thoughtless and reckless things to irritate our captive animals, especially in the outdoor gator exhibit where we kept nine, giant captive-raised alligators. A four foot high wooden fence surrounded them. Most of them were big enough to climb over the fence, but none of them wanted to do it. They had been raised in captivity, and knew no other kind of life. They were fed well, and kept clean. Even in the wild that's about all a gator really cares about.

The exhibit gators lay still for most of the day. They seldom moved about. Often a gator would lie right next to the fence. People could safely look over the fence at a huge gator right below them, and less than three feet away! Most visitors were content just to see a gator up close like that! And they took a lot of close up pictures!

But all too often some ignorant show off would not be satisfied with that arrangement! What puzzled and disappointed me the most was the fact that it was seldom a small child that would bother the gators. Most of the time, it was someone who should know better. It was usually a grown man! The excuse was always that everybody wanted to see it move, or see if it was alive! Sometimes some fool would climb the fence, break a branch off a bush, and run back to the gator exhibit just to poke a gator.

I collected a lot of pennies, quarters, and other coins that had been left on the heads of our captive gators. Every gator in that exhibit was marked with countless horrible scars that had been caused by a lighted cigarette left to burn out on their forehead. I could only imagine how painful that must have been for the gator!

We could not always catch the culprits in the act, but if I did happen to see anyone up to mischief, I would immediately act upon it!

If he had a stick I would forcibly confiscate it! I would tell him in no uncertain terms to "go out in the swamp and find his own gator to bully or torture! Leave mine alone!"

I also informed him that he just happened to be a guest in the largest Designated Wilderness Area east of the great Mississippi River! Everything living thing in the swamp is protected! Including the bush that the branch in his hand had come from! He had just committed a Federal Offense!

As long as he stayed in the park I would keep my eye on him.

If I caught him attempting to molest anything else, he would be forced to leave!

For more than fifty years Oscar was one of the main attractions, if not the main attraction at the Okefenokee Swamp Park!

Notes:

[1] After he passed away, Oscar's huge body was mounted by a taxidermist, and stands in a place of honor in the lobby of the interpretive center at the Okefenokee Swamp Park.
[2] My "gator call" was not very scientific. I merely yelled, "Here gator, gator, gator. Come on Boy!"
[3] Gators seldom take time out to enjoy a meal. They gulp it down as quickly as possible. It is doubtful that they even taste their food! They merely eat to survive! Most wild animals do that!
[4] My "Gator Pole" was a bamboo pole about six feet long with one end sanded smooth.

Part 2: Blind Suzy

One of our resident alligators was a nine foot female that had been given the name "Blind Suzy". Her left eye was missing, and she could barely see out of the right one. No one knows for sure how or when she lost her eye, but there was a lot of speculation going on about it.

Maybe someone shot it out, or maybe she lost it in a fight with another gator. Whatever the reason, Suzy did not seem to be even a little bit hindered without it. Although I often gave her a free fish, she hunted and caught most of her own food.

She had dug her 'gator hole' by a small pond out in back of the park where visitors were prohibited. During the winter months on cold days or nights, along with her offspring, that's where she spent most of her time.[1]

Suzy had lived in Oscar's territory for many years. She had

often mated with Oscar, and had become an expert at building her nest, and successfully hatching her young. Several times she produced as many as eleven tiny but healthy baby gators. Although she was a cold blooded reptile with an obviously primitive mindset, she was always surprisingly gentle with her offspring. Even to the extent of helping them to hatch out of their egg shells, gently taking them in her mighty jaws, and carefully transporting them to the water.

Her young would stay as close to her as they possibly could. Many a time two or three of them would be seen riding on their Momma's back. She did not feed them, but she would lead them to a spot where tadpoles or other tiny food items were readily available to them. She would stand guard over them like a mother hen! *God* help the intruder that threatened them!

By the end of their first year her young would have grown to a length of a foot or more. They would stay under her protection through that first year, and into the second year. In the winter they would follow her into her gator hole.

By the end of their second year most of the young would be over two feet long, and out on their own. There were always a few stragglers, unwilling to leave their mother's side. After numerous attempts to get them to leave on their own, she would resort to frightening them away. She would hiss and lunge at them fiercely. She would not harm them, but she would make them think she would, and eventually all of them would be gone.

By early summer of my first year as a park employee, I had become familiar with most of the resident gators. And by the same token they had become familiar with me. I had invented my own special "Okefenokee Joe gator call" and they had begun to readily respond to it. I had also learned how to reasonably imitate some of the sounds they make. For example I was pretty good at the muffled yelping grunt of a baby gator calling to its mom. I had learned to use that sound on occasions when I needed a gator to move or to come to me.

Blind Suzy had built a nest in her favorite spot near her gator hole out in back of the park. She had laid her eggs in it, and any day now they would begin to hatch. Most of her time for the past month or so had been spent on top of the nest, or near it, in an attempt to ward off any intruders.[2]

One morning I was out back hosing down the bear holding pens. From over near Suzy's nest I could hear what sounded like a baby gator calling. Thinking that maybe her eggs were hatching, I looked over, and standing across the small pond from Suzy's nest I saw a man I had never seen before. He was dressed in khakis. I was about to inform him that visitors were not allowed in the back of the park, when I noticed he had a pair of binoculars hanging around his neck, and a note pad and pencil in his hands. He looked pretty official. Apparently he was studying Suzy's nest. I thought to myself he must have permission to be there, and he might be someone important. So I walked over to speak to him. I said, "Hello!"

He didn't say a word. He just glanced over at me, with a look that probably meant, "Who the heck are you?" And he nodded a short impatient "hello" back at me. His attention immediately returned to Suzy's nest. I decided this was no time for carrying on a conversation with this man. So we both stood there in silence.

A moment later, lifting his binoculars, and looking through them at Suzy, he began once again to imitate a baby gator grunt. I could see what he was obviously trying to get some sort of reaction out of Suzy, and I couldn't help but ask him, "What are you trying to do?"

Without looking at me, he half way muttered in a bothered way, "I'm trying to get that gator to move off the nest, so I can see it!"

I stood there a while watching Suzy, and listening to the man grunt. Suzy was not budging, and I certainly did not want to insult the man, but I asked him, "Do you want me to try?"

With that same impatient look and in an irritable tone, he answered, "Sure! Go ahead, you try!"

I waited a moment; then in as loud a voice as I could muster, I belted out, "Suzy! Hup, hup!"

Immediately Suzy slid down off her nest into the water! And in one brief moment she had swum across the small pond, and on up the bank to us! We both had to jump back to keep from being knocked over by her!

We then introduced ourselves to one another, and to this day Howard hunt and I remain the best of friends![3]

As with all of our resident alligators Suzy would sometimes come out of the water, and lie on the paved walkway in close proximity to the tourists as they walked by. This of course was unnerving to our guests, and my standing orders in situations of that sort were to quickly move the alligator elsewhere. I had developed several different methods of moving them. It would depend on which resident gator it was that needed to be moved. For some of them, like Blind Suzy, I could just say the command, "Back in the water!" And usually she would readily obey.

Another easy method was to wave a fish in front of the gator, and slowly back up toward a safer place for the gator to be. The sight and smell of the fish would entice it to follow me. Then, making sure the gator was watching, I would throw the fish in the water, and the gator would go in after it. That is how I usually handled the moving of Oscar.

Other situations might call for more drastic measures, such as using my gator pole. I had discovered a certain "touchy" spot on the inside of both hind legs of an alligator. I would get behind the gator, and very gently tap those spots with the pole. This action would make the gator move. But it could only be done safely and successfully with the more reasonably tame resident gators.

Any one of these methods of moving an alligator was an exciting experience for our visitors to witness. People love to see alligators move.

It's a well-known fact that a female alligator will guard her nest while her eggs are incubating inside. What lengths she will go to in order to ward off an enemy varies from gator to gator. Initially, all expecting momma-gators will attempt to frighten all intruders away. She will stand up on her nest, or right next to it, hissing loudly, and position her body in a protective stance. She will look, and act as if she is ready to ferociously pounce on anything that gets near!

If this scare tactic on the part of the female does not work, and the intruder keeps coming, some females will abandon the nest. Some won't! Some will fight to the death to protect their eggs or their young! Since humans can never be sure which attitude a nest guarding alligator will assume, it is best to steer clear of all gator nests!

I can attest to the fact that Blind Suzy was one alligator that would stand and fight! She would, against all odds, definitely protect her young.[4]

One day I was standing on the little bridge out in front of the Serpentarium watching Jonas. The walkway on the bridge was about a foot above the water level of the canal. Suddenly Jonas surfaced, and began to swim hurriedly toward his safe haven, the old boat shelter! The next moment I discovered why he had left in such a hurry.

Suzy, with her mixed assembly of youngsters following her, was approaching. She was obviously taking her offspring out to the main park area for the day. There were eight of this year's model, and three of last year's model with her. She would slow down or stop every so often, to allow her stragglers to catch up to her.

As she passed under the bridge directly below me, I leaned over the railing, and spoke to her. I said,

"Hey, Suzy! That's a fine bunch of youngsters you've got with you!"

Suzy did not hesitate for a second! Without making a sound she lunged up at me with her mouth wide open! Her whole body came up out of the water, except for her tail! I felt a mighty rush of air, as her jaws slammed shut right in front of my face! That was a close call! Had I been leaning any further over that railing she quite possibly could have grabbed me by my head!

Needless to say, from that time on, if I saw her with her young, I made sure that I never got that close to her again!

During the warmer months, Suzy and her offspring would 'hangout' around the main park area. Visitors could see her with her family, and get close enough to take pictures of them. She and her young were always quite an attraction! Off and on, during the day, I would toss her a fish! That is probably the reason she would stay nearby.

Notes:

[1] A gator hole can be a spot where the gator has dug a deep hole in the muck at the bottom of a body of water, and made the water deeper. Or it can be a narrow tunnel dug into the bank of a body of water. The tunnel is not very deep and seldom more than twenty feet long. The entrance is just wide enough for the gator to enter. The rear of the tunnel is widened so that the gator is able to turn completely around. Except in the case of females with their young, it is usually occupied only by the gator that dug it. It serves as winter quarters for the gator, and in times of drought, a haven for fish and other aquatic swamp life.

[2] A gator nest is a mound about four or five feet tall, and five or six feet wide at the bottom. It is pyramid shaped. It is made of mud, twigs, leaves, bark, and whatever the female can find that is suitable. When the time comes she will dig out part of it, and lay her eggs in it. She'll cover them up, and stand guard over the nest. She does not incubate them. Nature, with the aid of heat from the decaying matter in the mound, does that!

[3] Over the years Howard Hunt has done many studies, and written many scientific papers on the American alligator. His valuable contributions have done much to bring to the scientific community a broader understanding of the American alligator.

[4] According to my friend Howard Hunt the main predators of gator nests are the American black bear, and the raccoon.

Part 3: Jonas

I had been working at the park for almost a year when I began noticing a strange bull gator hanging around in the canal in front of the Serpentarium. It was over ten feet long. Most of the time it kept its body under the dark tea colored water, and all I could see of it was its nose, and its eyes. I could not help but notice something very different about its eyes. They seemed a bit clearer, and there seemed to be a more intelligent look about them than the other resident gators.

My guess was that it was a wild gator fresh in from the swamp, and it was probably hiding from Oscar. It stayed in the water most of the time, and I assumed that it did that so it could swim away quickly. I named it Jonas.

It soon became obvious that this 'new' gator was definitely a little more intelligent than the others. It was a fast learner, and quick to respond to the few commands I would give it. I decided to train it to do more or less the same tricks that Oscar, our largest resident gator, had been doing for many years. Our visitors always enjoyed his short alligator shows.

I made use of the training periods of Jonas for the entertainment benefit of the crowd. Before each lesson, I would make sure that all the people within the sound of my voice would hear my famous "Okefenokee Joe Gator Call", and gather around us. When they did, I would explain to them that I was about to bring Jonas closer to us, and where they should stay to safely enjoy our short little show. Of course, Jonas had been alerted by my gator call, too, and had swum over toward me. Then, with a small fish in my hand, I would wave at Jonas and say his name. I added the command, "Hup, hup!" and if he swam closer to me to get his fish, I'd throw it into the water near him. He would then submerge and hunt for it.

An alligator cannot turn its head without its whole body turning with it. And as Jonas searched for the fish, he would demonstrate that fact. It was interesting to the public to see his whole body turn in the shallow water, as he groped for the fish with his open jaws. He would always find it, and when he did he usually would inadvertently grab a mouthful of mud and vegetation along with it. The audience would see him lift his head up out of the water, and gulp the whole sloppy mess down in just a few swallows.

He wasted no time chewing or enjoying the taste of his meal. He usually took it all down in just one or two mighty gulps, and the crowd would be thrilled to see it! Our visitors really enjoyed that short gator show. Those who had cameras took many photographs of the action. Unbeknownst to them I was actually collecting data on alligator behavior, while at the same, time training my super intelligent gator to perform for them.

After the applause died down, I would mention to my audience that the 'show' was over, and I hoped they would enjoy the rest of their day at the park. The crowd would then disburse. Sometimes when I called him over to me, he would open his mouth, and instead of throwing the fish in the water, I would throw it directly to him. He would often catch it in his mouth, and swallow it! Occasionally he would try to catch it and miss. Then he would have to hunt for it. No matter what the outcome, the crowd loved to see the show!

After several weeks of calling him to me, and giving him a fish in the water, I began attempting to bring him out of the water, and up onto the bank of the canal. That way the people would get to see his whole body, and watch him move.

Treats are by far the best method to train any wild animal. An alligator is no exception to that rule. I would call to him, and offer him a fish. But I did not toss it in the water when he came near. Making sure he was watching me, I would lay it down on the bank of the canal. I would give him the "Hup, hup" command and move a short distance away. He soon learned that in order to get his treat he would have to come out of the water, and up on the bank to get it.

In just a few short days I found that it was no longer necessary to wave a fish at him to get him up. All I had to do was call him, and give the command, "Hup, hup" and he would come up out of the water to me.

And I would say, "Down!"

And just as Oscar had learned to do, he would stop where he was and settle down flat on his belly. Then, for the benefit of the audience, I would tap him on the nose with a fish. He would open up his jaws as wide as he could, and I would carefully toss the fish into his mouth. Often in one crunchy gulp he would swallow it![1]

I'd give the crowd time to take a few pictures. Then Jonas would receive the only other command I would ever give him,

"Swampwise"

which was, "Back in the water!" This was also the only command that he would sometimes take too long a time to obey. And, for the safety of the visitors, it was the most important order for him to follow. I learned that, if necessary, I could hurry him in any direction with the use of my 'gator pole'. It was a bamboo poll about five feet long with the end rounded off. With it I could gently poke at one or the other of his rear legs, and he would move a few feet in the direction he needed to go. It depended how far he was from the water, as to how many gentle pokes he would receive. For the safety of our visitors, I always coaxed him back into the water, before I left the scene.[2]

Notes:

[1] This was the same show that Oscar had been performing for years at the park. Now we had two resident gators that would do it. Invariably one or the other would always be available to call upon to do a short show for our visitors.

[2] Sometimes, when it was necessary to move a gator, and if my 'gator pole' was not handy, I would get behind the gator, and poke its rear legs with my hand. I always made sure I was on balance, and ready to move in any direction or jump away from the gator if it became necessary.

Part 4: Jonas and the Rattler

The little bridge over the canal in front of the serpentarium was a perfect spot from which to observe wild life. I would often see Jonas out there in the water waiting patiently for whatever the day might bring. Most of the time, just his nose and his eyes were visible because he would keep his body under water. I suppose he felt safer that way. I could also see Oscar's Island from the bridge.

One morning I had stopped on the bridge to say hello to Jonas when a familiar movement in the Maiden Cane on the far bank of the canal caught my eye. A deadly canebrake rattlesnake had crawled out of the swamp, and was drinking water from the canal! The snake was about four feet long. Since part of my job was to remove dangerous wild animals from the main park area of the park, I was obligated to capture that snake, and transport it elsewhere.

I hurried to the Serpentarium, grabbed my snake hook and an empty carrying box! Then I rushed back outside, and ran to the spot where I had last seen the snake! It must have sensed me coming, because it had slipped into the water, and was swimming toward the opposite bank of the canal! Jonas had also spotted it, and was swimming rapidly after it! I was about to witness yet another once in a lifetime wildlife scene!

Jonas opened his jaws and caught the snake in the middle of its body! He shook it violently for a few seconds! I could hear the sickening sound of its head and its rattles slapping the water, and smacking Jonas on either side of his huge head! Then he quickly dropped it into the water! I had never seen an alligator so rapidly shake something like that! He grabbed it again, and this time he chewed on it as he shook it. The rattlesnake's body had grown limp. I could see both its head and its tail hanging lifelessly from those powerful tooth filled jaws. It was probably dead, but apparently Jonas was not going to take any chances. He repeated that same maneuver over and over again, shaking it and chewing it! Finally he dropped it in the water and just watched it. It didn't move! It just lay there lifeless, floating on the surface of the water. Jonas waited a little longer, and then one final time he took it in his jaws! He lifted his head up, and as gators sometimes do, in several huge gulps he swallowed it.

With the rattlesnake gone, although Jonas had done it for me, my job was done. The visitors were safe, and Jonas had a full belly!

Part 5: Alligator Territorial Rights

The big bull alligator reining over its territory always exhibits great tolerance. Every wild creature in the swamp is welcome to come in and live in its kingdom, except for one. That would be another bull gator.

One morning I was surprised to see Jonas up on the bank of the canal. That was unusual, because he spent most of his time in the water, with just his nose and his eyes visible. He was always hiding from Oscar. Several excited tourists had broken a standard park rule, and had walked off the paved walkway. They were gathered close around Jonas, watching him, and photographing him.

Suddenly a movement in the water over by Oscar's Island caught my eye! It was Oscar, and he was swimming swiftly in our direction. He had not smacked the water with his body as he usually did when he was after Jonas. For some reason, this time, without making a sound, he had just slid into the water.

It was obvious that for some reason this time Jonas was unaware of his approach. Fearing for his safety, and for the safety of our visitors, I knew I must do something, and do it fast! So I yelled, "Everybody please get back on the walkway! Jonas! Back in the water!"

No one moved, including Jonas! So I repeated, "Everybody, please get back on the pavement, and Jonas back in the water!"

This time the people did move, partly because of the urgency in my voice, and partly because they were horrified to see Oscar twenty feet away and coming up out of the water straight toward them! He was after Jonas, and the group was in his way!

They had moved off just in time because Jonas, now also aware that Oscar was so close and he was about to be attacked, moved swiftly across the ground and into the water. If the tourists had stayed where they had been, in his haste, he most certainly would have knocked several of them down. And with Oscar chasing so closely after Jonas, they would have been trampled by him, also!

By the time Oscar reached the water, Jonas had swum a good distance under the water back towards the old boat shelter. Oscar frantically searched the area unsuccessfully. He stayed there on 'guard duty' most of the day. Once again Jonas had escaped his wrathful clutches!

Jonas was not always that lucky. One afternoon, during gator mating season, I heard Oscar slam the water. I ran up on the little bridge to get a better look. Jonas had already submerged, and the bubbles he was making told me that instead of heading for the old boat shelter where he would be safe, he was moving the other way. I'll never know why he chose to go that way. He must have known that in less than thirty yards, in the direction he was swimming, the canal came to a dead end. From there on he would have to travel on dry land to get away from Oscar!

But Jonas never got that far. Oscar had caught him by the tail, and with a mighty lunge he turned him over on his back! In a desperate attempt to break Oscar's grip Jonas turned his upside down body completely around and grabbed Oscar's right rear leg! Holding each other in that manner, together they rolled over and over in the water. They were not biting or tearing at each other, they were just holding on, and rolling! Neither one uttered a sound. All that was heard was the crashing of their bodies, the splashing of the water, and the screams of the now terrified tourists! Otherwise the battle was done in silence.

Finally Oscar let go. When he did Jonas also released his grip on Oscar's leg. He submerged, and began to swim under water, faster than I would have dreamed possible, toward the old boat shelter. Oscar did not follow him. The battle was over, and no serious wounds had been inflicted on either combatant![1]

Notes:

[1] I was learning that battles between wild animals of the same species seldom, if ever, end in the death of either combatant. If death does occur it is by mistake. I believe that one explanation for that is the simple fact that

such battles are never fought over the things humans fight over. Such as anger, jealousy, envy, greed, hate, etc.

Part 6: Observations of Alligator Intelligence

My observations and experiences had been teaching me first-hand many interesting facts about the attitudes and behaviors of all wild animals, especially the alligators. Before Jonas came along, I had no idea how remarkably keen the senses of an alligator really are. Much of what he was showing me could not be found in books.

He was the first to demonstrate to me an almost unbelievable sense that possibly not all of them possess. But he certainly did! It is an important sense, vital to his survival. And this is how he taught it to me.

One afternoon, as usual, Jonas was in his favorite spot in the canal in front of the serpentarium. When I called to him he turned his body completely around, and faced me. I didn't have a fish with me, but by now we had become somewhat acquainted, and he would follow most of my few short commands without any promise of a reward. I was actually calling to him just to say hello. I did that often during the day.

Across the main park area, about one hundred yards away, I saw Oscar stretched out comfortably on his little island. He looked as if he was at peace with the world, and completely satisfied with life, and I said to Jonas, "Hey, my swampwise friend! It's a good thing that big guy doesn't know you are here!"

I spent the next few minutes just admiring Jonas, and talking to him. I was always amazed at how intelligent he seemed to be, compared to most of the other resident gators.

Suddenly he submerged, and vanished under the dark 'tea colored' water! Then a mighty thump and a heavy splash caught my attention! Automatically I quickly looked in the direction that the sound had come from! A bolt of shocking realization went through me! Oscar had left his island!

I knew full well what was about to transpire! Oscar was coming after Jonas again! I stood there on the little bridge watching the bubbles appearing on the surface of the water, telling me where Jonas was going! He was swimming, as fast as he could, underwater towards the tributary canal that led to the park's old boat shelter, a good distance away.

Oscar was swimming rapidly toward us, and in just a few minutes he arrived on the scene where Jonas had been! He was not making a sound, but he was frantically, almost fanatically searching the area! Obviously he was looking for Jonas! But by now Jonas was nowhere near.

Unable to locate his quarry, Oscar finally calmed down. He remained in the area, silently watching, and waiting for the remainder of the day. Naturally, as long as Oscar was nearby, Jonas stayed in the safe haven of the old boat shelter.

How did Oscar know that Jonas was in the canal by the Serpentarium? The distance between them was at least one hundred yards, and covered with vegetation. Neither of them could possibly have seen one another. I could see them both simply because I was at a higher elevation on that little bridge. Could it be that Oscar heard me talking to Jonas? That was unlikely. I was too far away. Or was I? How did Jonas know that Oscar was coming? He had submerged a few seconds before I heard that loud thump that Oscar had made! How had Jonas become aware of Oscar's intent before he did that?

Could they have smelled the presence of one another? Possibly, but that would not explain how Jonas knew ahead of time that Oscar was going to dive in the water, and come after him. For me, this was the beginning of my education into the inexplicable, telepathic sense that some alligators and certain other wild animals seem to possess.

It should be noted here that there were many times when Jonas did not become aware of Oscar's approach before hand, and didn't get out of his way in time. So whatever the sense may be, it could not be counted upon, because it obviously does not always work.

As the days went by, I began spending more time observing Jonas. He was not always visible, but when he was I would experiment with him. I was learning that although an alligator's brain is no bigger than a half dollar, its power of association is more than equal to that of most German Shepherd dogs!

Many times I would spot Jonas lying in the water, not looking my way. Just to see what his reaction might be, without using my special gator call, I would whisper his name. I found that I could be as much as two hundred feet away from him, and at my whisper he would turn and look my way. I also tried the same maneuver with both Oscar and Blind Suzy, with the same significant result. I would carry it even further by whispering, "Hup, hup" and each of them would swim over toward me. I began to understand that an alligator's sense of hearing is remarkably acute!

I also learned that alligators can be taught to understand, and obey certain hand signals. For example, without saying a word I could wave my hands, using the motion that we humans interpret as "come here", and each of our resident gators would come to me. If I motioned for them to lie down, they would do it!

Sometimes, in the morning, I would place a fresh fish on the bank of a canal, and cover it with leaves so it would not be seen. Every now and then a raccoon or an American egret would beat the gator to it. But most of the time an alligator would get the fish, and it was its sense of smell that helped it do it. Collectively, the alligators of the Okefenokee Swamp were demonstrating that their senses were equal to, or better than those of their wild animal neighbors.

I came up with an idea to test them in another way. Oscar was sunning himself on his island. He was lying there comfortably with his body stretched out, and his chin resting on the ground. I got behind him so that his tail was facing me, and his head was pointing the other way. I was at least fifty yards away from him. Just to see what would happen, without saying a word, I made the 'come here' motion. To my astonishment he immediately raised his head, turned his body around, and looked my way. He did not move toward me, but somehow he had known I was there, and that I was motioning to him!

My first thought about what I had just seen was that he really didn't see me waving my arms. Possibly it was just a coincidence that he turned around just at that precise moment. Keeping that thought in mind, I decided to experiment further. Over the next few days and weeks I tried the same trick dozens of times with all the resident alligators in the park. Believe it or not they all showed the same remarkable ability to see directly behind themselves without turning around. Even at a great distance they would react to movement behind them!

I began to wonder about that extra sense I had noted that day when Jonas somehow knew Oscar was coming for him, before Oscar had even moved! Could it be that wild animals possess a certain sense that we humans are not yet aware of? And why would it work sometimes, and not other times?

Part 7: My Gator Scar

One morning on Jekyl Island, Georgia, shortly after sun up, I was carrying my crab basket, with my cast net tucked inside, a long handled crab net in my left hand, and several baited crab poles in my right. And of course my salt water skinning knife was in a sheath on my belt.[1]

It was a beautiful calm day. As a hunter I always like days with not much wind. I have noticed that wind, like a full moon, spooks all wild animals. It upsets their normal routine. I have learned that to be true even of the creatures that live in the water. Right at the full moon, though, I had learned that the blue crabs were at their peak in their monthly growing cycle, which meant that they were full of meat! This was the first day of the full moon, and I was looking forward to a good catch of fully developed big blue crabs!

"Swampwise"

I was heading for my favorite crabbing hole. The going was slow because the water was about ankle deep, and the muck beneath it was sucking at my old tennis shoes. In some places I was slowed down even further, because the marsh grass was chest high, and I couldn't see more than a foot or two in front of me. I was using the crab poles to move the grass to the side, so I could safely see where I was putting my feet, and where I was going. The common sense of swamp wisdom had taught me to be careful not to put my hands or feet anywhere without first checking to see what is there. In other words, I should never step on anything I shouldn't step on! That's swampwise!

I was suddenly surprised when I saw a part of the tail of an alligator just a foot or two in front of me. I moved the grass a little more, and I saw the rest of its body. It was whole alligator, about six feet long, and it was lying there out in the marsh, at least forty feet from the water. I thought to myself, "Now that gator could not possibly be alive! A live alligator would have heard me coming, and be long gone before I got near it! And what in the world would an alligator be doing, lying way out there in the marsh? It doesn't make sense! It must be dead!"

So I decided to find out what had happened to it. I put my poles, my net, and my basket on the ground, and reached down to pick it up by the tail and turn it over. The second I touched its tail that gator came alive! It turned around, with its mouth wide open, and before I was able to move, it grabbed me by the neck and part of my chest, and hung on! It was trying to roll with me, but neither one of us was positioned right! The shock and the pain were sent running through me like a rocket! So did the fear!

Part survival instinct and part alligator knowledge took over, and I quickly poked both of my thumbs forcefully into each of its ear openings on the sides of its head! *Thank God* it immediately turned me loose, and backed off! It was about five feet away from me, looking straight at me, and giving out with that loud threatening hissing sound that gator's make when they are frightened or concerned! Prior to all of this the gator had not made a sound!

It lay there at bay, standing its ground! For some reason,

known only to the gator, it was not attempting to escape from me. With my neck and chest throbbing, and my eyes on that gator, I very carefully picked up my equipment, and slowly moved away from the gator, and back toward my jeep. It just lay there watching me, and hissing.

About thirty feet away I stopped and stood there for a moment contemplating on what to do next. Since the pain was subsiding and there was not much blood from the deep scratches in my chest, I decided not to go to the emergency ward at the hospital in Brunswick. Making a wide detour around that gator, I continued my journey to the creek. I was not going to let that gator scare me out of a good day's catch of seafood![2]

After that near tragedy, It turned out to be a good day! I had gathered the usual half bushel of clams, a couple dozen nice blue claw crabs, and several large smoking size mullets.

That wild, Jekyl Island gator put a deep scar on my chest that for the rest of my life will serve me as a reminder of the alligator safety lesson it taught me that day!

Notes:

[1] My crab poles were six feet long, and one inch in diameter. One end was sharpened so that it could easily be sunk into the muck of the creek bottom, and the pole would stand upright. Twelve feet of strong nylon cord was tied to the other end, and wrapped around it. My crab bait was a fresh piece of chicken, usually the leg, tied to the end of the cord. I'd toss the baited line into the water. Sooner or later a hungry crab would grab it. Then it was a fantastically, exciting thrill to patiently and slowly pull the line toward me and my waiting crab net. If done right the crab will usually hold on to the bait long enough to get the net up under it, and capture it!

[2] Always, when I was in the water catching my food, I kept an eye out for any danger. In that respect, this day I was even more wary. I kept an eye out for that gator the whole five hours I was in the water, and enjoying the catch. The feast that night, and for the next few days, was worth all the danger and the effort of the day!

"Swampwise"

Part 8: Why Do Gators Bellow?

As long as I live I will remember the first time I ever heard an alligator bellow! It was Oscar, and I didn't just hear him bellow! From less than twenty feet from him, I watched him do it!

It was a typically calm spring afternoon. I had been working at the Okefenokee Swamp Park for less than a week. Oscar, our giant resident alligator, was enjoying the comfort of the sun on his back, as he lay there on his island, seemingly at peace with the world.

Then, as if he had just remembered something extremely important, he raised his head up off the ground, and took a deep breath. With his belly on the ground, his head slightly raised and his jaws partially open, he let out with a terrific honest to goodness, alligator bellow! I know it was just my imagination, but it felt as if the ground all around me was shaking! The sound of that bellow added one more reason to the long list of reasons why Oscar was most definitely the king of the swamp!

During my years in the Okefenokee, I heard many an alligator bellow. I was surprised to learn that even tiny alligators bellow. Males and females alike, in the water or up on land, wherever they happen to be, if they feel the urge they will bellow.

Because I was so deeply interested in wild animal behavior, I kept almost daily notes on what I'd see and hear regarding my captive wild animals, and the truly wild ones. I have one notation written back in the 70's. It says,"I was camping on an eighteen thousand acre deer hunting plantation in South Carolina in April. I heard an alligator bellowing in a pond not far from my tent. It was three o'clock in the morning, the temperature was a chilling forty three degrees, and it was raining. Now why in the world would an alligator bellow under those conditions?

Much scientific data has been collected on the meaning of the bellow, but because any answer is merely speculation, no scientific explanation or conclusion is possible.

To clear the matter up, I have written this song poem! It is called "Why Do Gators Bellow?" It can be sampled, downloaded or purchased as with all of my recordings, at my website; www.okefenokeejoe.com

Why do Gators Bellow?
A Song by Okefenokee Joe

The scream of a tiny screech owl is an awesome fearful sound
It'll raise the hair straight up on end of the bravest man around
If a panther squalls on a dark night, it
can cause your heart to pound
But when a big bull gator bellows, it can even shake the ground

Why do gators bellow, why do they make that sound?
Are they just feelin' mellow, are they just foolin' 'round
Is there some special reason why the
swamp should so resound?
Why do gators bellow, why do they make that sound?

They bellow in the winter, summer, spring and fall
Males, and females, big and small, they bellow one and all
Sometimes it's just one single gator, callin' from it's lair
And then sometimes a thunderin' chorus rumbles everywhere

Why do gators bellow, why do they make that sound?
The season's not the reason, we hear 'em all year 'round
Are they markin' territory, or callin' mates so they'll be found
Why do gators bellow, why do they make that sound?

It means the weather's turnin', or the fish won't bite today
It could mean your luck's about to change,
that's what old timers say
Is it the barometric pressure, the temperature, or the time
Scientists are bewildered, nothin' seems to rhyme

"Swampwise"

I've pondered on this subject half my life and more
Each time I think I've learned the truth, I know less than before
Could it be that they're just feelin' good, and spreadin' it around
Why do gators bellow, why do they make that sound?

Perhaps it's just a gator thing, we can put no meanin' to
And the answer is, it's simply somethin' gators like to do

© 2016 Black Water Music Co., BMI

CHAPTER 9
WHY SNAKES?

Part 1: Overcoming the fear

Believe it or not I grew up in Philadelphia, Pennsyvania. As everyone knows "Philly" is a gigantic, and thoroughly modern city. The name that was given to me at birth is Richard Edmond Flood, and of course my nickname was simply Dick. My high school football coach, and team mates called me "Floody". In most ways I was just an another average kid on the block. I suppose the fact that I turned out as I did in later life, is a story worth telling. I did not become "Swampwise" or "Okefenokee Joe" overnight!

I remember, after I had learned how to read, my very first and most favorite book was written by Edgar Rice Burroughs. It was called *Tarzan of the Apes*. There was a whole series of Tarzan books, and eventually I had them all. I read them all over and over again.

The character of Tarzan, that Mr. Burroughs had invented, stood for all the righteous aspects of human character that most decent, *God*-fearing, and lawful human beings strive for: honesty, integrity, loyalty, bravery, tolerance, faithfulness, generosity, forgiveness, and so on.

Although he was supposedly raised in the jungle by a band of wild gorillas, Tarzan lived by all the rules of human decency! Those books truly influenced me in many ways as a child. I wanted to be just like Tarzan! I wanted to possess all the good qualities he so heroically portrayed. And just as he was friends with most every animal in the jungle, I wanted to be friends with the animals in the woods around my neighborhood. I wanted to climb trees! And I wanted to be brave, courageous, and bold, like Tarzan!

The one thing I was not so sure about was the fact that Tarzan had a scar on his face that turned red when he was mad! I was not very keen about getting my head cut, so I'd have a scar too. Besides that, I was not sure, how in the world, I could make it turn red!

Back in the early 1940s there were still a lot of unmapped areas all over the United States. And there was one huge seven thousand acre or more vacant lot within several blocks of my house! I lived in a section of the city known as Germantown. There were actually deer, raccoons, opossums, an occasional bobcat, and other small furry creatures living in that vacant lot. And there were snakes! Yep! There were snakes!

I'm not sure how old I was when I first began to venture into that vacant lot. Usually my friends were afraid to go in there with me, so I went alone. My parents warned me not to do it. They were mostly concerned about me meeting up with what everyone around my neighborhood called the "Railroad Bums." They were the grubby, foul-smelling men that hung around in the caves next to the railroad tracks. A few of them were down and out wounded military vets that had been discharged during the early days of World War two. And I did get to know some of them. I kept myself always on the "ready to run mode," but never did I have any trouble with any of them.

The poor fellows did not have money enough to buy real liqueur. They would go to a drug store, and for a few pennies they could buy a cheap bottle of a product on the market, that contained a minute amount of alcohol. The name of it was Witch Hazel. They would stay all "liquored up' on that stuff, and most of the time they were so far out of it, that it was difficult, and sometimes just about impossible to talk to any of them. It eventually probably killed a lot of them. The label on the bottle said "Harmful & possibly fatal if swallowed".

I know now that I never should have done it, but I'd go home and pull a pack of cigarettes out of my daddy's carton of Camels! I'd take some slices of bread out of the family's bread box, and some oranges, cans of soup, or whatever I thought I could get away with, and I would take it all to my bum friends. I even took them matches!

Thinking about it now, I realize that much of the time they were too far gone to appreciate what I was doing. And every now and then, when I look back, I kick myself for sometimes spending most of my allowance to buy those guys a bottle of Witch hazel. I know now it was not good for them. Back then it did not cross my mind.

Drunk as they were, sometimes the stories they would tell me about the war had my hair standing up on end. And all of them, at one time or another gave me the same sound advice. They told me to "Never join the army"!

There were several creeks running through that vacant lot. The water was pretty dirty from the trash and garbage that people so often thoughtlessly dumped out there. It was against the law to do that, but they did it anyhow. Just like now a days. I guess there will always be a few slobs around. Maybe it's just human nature?

One afternoon I had said goodbye to my "bum" friends, and I was walking along a creek bed just enjoying being in the woods. All of a sudden, ahead of me a cottontail rabbit seemed to come from out of nowhere, and hopped across the creek. That really startled me! And almost immediately, right at my feet an entire covey of quail flew up off the ground! It all took me totally by surprise! I was a young inexperienced kid, and the sudden, and unexpected sound of wings flapping, and all those small brown creatures seemingly exploding into the air right in front of me, scared me! But that's not all that got to me!

The excitement had caused me to trip over an old empty wooden orange crate! The crate moved a little with me, when I fell over it, and as I started to push myself back up off the ground a huge but harmless garter snake slithered over my left hand, right next to my face! It must have come out from under the crate

"Swampwise"

when I moved it! It went on up the creek bank, and disappeared into the thick foliage.

That snake scared me out of my wits! It was the first real live snake I had ever seen out in the woods! A real, honest to goodness wild one! I know now, of course, that a garter snake is not venomous, and does not pose a serious threat to any human. But back then I had not learned much about anything. All I knew was I wanted to be in the woods, and I wanted to be like Tarzan!

I have honestly wondered ever since that day, why I was so frightened. It didn't try to hurt me. It crawled over my hand simply because my hand was in its way, in its attempt to escape from me. To this day I still wonder what had caused that terrible few seconds of almost paralizing fear over a snake.

But, believe it or not, that fear is one of the basic reasons that caused me to do what I do, and to be who I am today! I wanted to get over that fear. And as I was getting over it, I couldn't help but begin to get into snakes! They are actually beautiful, and fascinating! I'll admit though, that back then there was also another reason I wanted to get over my fear of snakes. Possibly a better reason!

There was a sweet little girl who lived down the block from me. She was beautiful, and I was deeply in love with her. The trouble was she was two years older than me, and she liked my older brother.

When kids are growing up, two years difference between a girl and a boy is like thirty, or more. I was too young for her, and I was sure she would never even notice me. We knew each other simply because we were neighbors. And I was too shy to even try to be more than friends with her.

One day I saw her out in her back yard. As I walked by her gate, I noticed she had a cigar box in her hand. I had a lump in my throat as big as a mountain just seeing her there, but I managed to blurt out,

"Hi Sue! What's in the box?"

She said, "It's Wiggles"!

And I asked her, "What is Wiggles?"

She answered, "Come on over, and see for yourself!"

I was so excited! She didn't need to ask me twice! I was over that fence in a second, and by her side! She carefully opened the cigar box, and held it towards me, so I could see inside. I noticed that the lid to the cigar box had several holes in it. I assumed that they were air holes. In the box the only thing I saw was a small, flat rock! I said to her, "It's just a stone from the creek! Are you playing a joke on me?"

She answered me by reaching into the box, and gently pulling the little rock out. Then she again held it out to me, so I could see inside.

Neatly coiled up on its sawdust bottom was a pretty, harmless little red black and yellow scarlet king snake! It was about ten inches long. Her dad, who was a doctor, had ordered it for her from a pet store. I could not believe how strikingly beautiful it was! Bold and shiny bright red, black, and yellow bands surrounded its body.

Temporarily all fear of snakes left me immediately! If the woman I loved could keep a snake for a pet, then there is no way I'm gonna' show her I am afraid of them!

She brought it out of the box, and the first thing I noticed was that it was not biting her. Then she held it toward me, and offered to let me hold it! Trying desperately not to let her see how I was shaking in my boots, for the first time in my life, I held a snake in my bare hands!

That was a long time ago. It played a serious role in my thoughts of snakes! I was nine years old and the final "no going back now" convincing reason for my avid interest in them came to me that summer!

Part 2: Memories of Camp Carson

At the age of nine I talked my parents into letting me go to a YMCA camp, in the mountains of Pennsylvania, for two weeks. It cost them to let me do that, but they knew how much I loved the outdoors, and since it was a Christian-based organization, they thought it might do me some good spiritually.

It was my first time away from home, and after two days, for some reason, I guess it was homesickness, I wanted to come home. I wrote, and told my folks that. They wrote back, telling me that they would be up on the weekend to get me. The camp was about ninety miles from my house. I gritted my teeth and steeled myself to the fact that I just had to wait another day or so, and I'd be home.

About an hour after I had read their letter, I was down by the lake skimming small flat stones across the water. Little cricket frogs were jumping all around at my feet. I started trying to catch one, when I saw a northern banded water snake swimming along the bank. Of course I did not know then, what kind of a snake it was, but I did know that it was not a venomous copperhead. I thought of that beautiful scarlet king snake my neighborhood crush had for a pet. That pretty little snake would not bite anyone. And thinking that the water snake might make a good pet for me, like a dummy I reached down and grabbed it by the tail.

As I pulled it out of the water, it turned and nailed me a good one on my hand! I was surprised that it did not hurt, and in fright more than pain, I immediately dropped it!

I watched it swim away to safety, and I got to thinking. It was probably scared of me, because it did not know me. Thats why it bit me! At the same time I realized that the most important thing to know about a bite from a harmless snake is that it does not hurt a bit! The teeth of all our non-venomous snakes are tiny, and mean't only for holding, not chewing.

Although it drew a small amount of blood it was not at all painful! And besides that, maybe the next time I see one, I'll be more careful, and catch it behind its head, so it couldn't bite me.

Then I would let it get to know me, before I'd try to play with it. I was more intrigued and interested than frightened. So I began to look along the edge of the lake for another water snake. I also began to do something else. I began to forget that I wanted to go home!

Saturday arrived, and my folks drove up to the camp to bring me home. They were just a little upset that I had decided to stay, but they were glad to see me. We turned the "take me home trip" into a visiting day. That afternoon they drove home without me. And that evening, during the free play period, just before dark, down by the lake, I caught my first water snake!

In the nature lodge at the camp there were several snake cages. One of them was empty, and the counselor in charge allowed me to keep my new pet in it. He also gave me a lot of tips on how to care for a snake in captivity. I learned to keep the cage clean, and dry, keep its water bowl full, when and what to feed it, and just good common snake care sense, and know how.

By the time my first two weeks was up at the camp, I had pulled a complete switch in my feelings. I was now crying because I did not want to leave! After my folks got me home, I pestered them so much about it, that they reserved me the last two week period at the camp that summer!

During those last two weeks of my first summer at the camp, the YMCA had hired a special speaker to join us at our once a week Saturday night council fire. That was the special night when the entire camp would gather in the council circle.

The guest speaker was a full blood Lakota Indian! He called himself "Chief Sunrise". He told stories of the old ways, and he would play a hand drum, and sing Lakota songs. Those songs, and that drum beat woke up something primitive inside me, that as old as I am now, has still not gone back to sleep! It's a feeling that I have never been able to explain—a restless longing for some unexplainable thing that just isn't there. My daddy called it, "The call of the wild". And I believe he was absolutely correct!

That summer was the real clincher. I was hooked forever on American Indian lore, the snakes, camping, and the outdoors in general! It also started me on the path to a much deeper understanding, and appreciation of *God*'s work in the natural world around us!

Part 3: My First Real Snake Hunt

The camp bugler at Camp Carson was into snake hunting. I don't know if he liked snakes or not, but he loved to hunt them, and he'd kill them. He had a lot of cured copperhead skins hanging over his bunk. He had cured them himself.

At first the camp director thought I was too young to go up the mountain with that fellow after copperheads. But this was my second year as a camper. I was ten years old, and he saw how well I handled snakes at the nature lodge, and he decided it was ok.

There were three of us. Since I was the youngest, and the novice, I brought up the rear. On up "Little Mountain" we went! As we got closer to the top, where the copperhead den was, the pace slowed. I was cautioned once more about being careful, and not to step on one.

There is a saying amongst hunters and outdoorsmen. They say, "It's always the third guy in line that gets snake bit!"

Knowing now what I have learned about snakes that saying makes plenty of sense to me. And because I believe that the greatest danger regarding our venomous snakes is that the snake more than likely will be unaware of your approach, and fail to move out of your way. All wild animals know this, and they watch out. People need to do the same thing. Because I consider that to be the number one greatest danger I always brought up that subject in all of my presentations.

Well guess what? I was the third guy in line, and I didn't get bitten, but I did find the first copperhead! The other two older and more experienced hunters had walked right on by it! It probably came out more as a scream, but I hollered, "Snake! I think it's a copperhead!"

They both came, running back to where I was! One of them immediately pinned that little snake's head down brutally against the rocks, and with his knife, he quickly, and without ceremony cut off its head! He picked up the still wriggling and bloody body, and handed it to me, saying, "You found him! You skin him!"

I took the dead snake from him, but I remember thinking, "This is snake hunting? It's pretty vicious! I don't know if I like doing this."

That little copperhead was lying there in the rocks minding its own business. I felt sorry for it, and I wasn't so sure I wanted to hunt snakes with these guys anymore.

They taught me how to skin the snake. We tacked it down on a flat board, covered it with table salt, and set it out in the sun. We'd bring it in at night to keep the dew from getting it. The skin had to stay pinned like that, with salt on it, for at least three days, and then it would be cured. It would be as stiff as a board, but it was cured. As I grew older I did a lot of trapping, and I learned several new and more efficient ways to properly tan a hide.

Part 4: American Indian Influence

There was an honor society at Camp Carson. It was called Tatanka. This is the Lakota word meaning buffalo. Its members were responsible for several of the camp's night time events, around the campfire. I was completely awed by the ceremonies that the members would perform. Even though I knew that they were all white guys dressed as Indians, It was the meaning, and the representation of an old way of life that impressed me. At my tender age I was fast becoming interested in living off the land, as the Indians did, and in wilderness survival!

To become a member of Tatanka, a camper had to be in at least his second year at the camp. Each age group would vote

"Swampwise"

for the person in their group that they deemed the best all-around and likeable camper. The initiation period lasted three days, and nights. I learned that Tatanka's every by law, and ceremony came from the knowledge gained in the authenticity of Dr. Charles Eastman's, (a full blooded Lakota Indian) books. I know this because in my second year at Camp Carson, at the age of ten, I became a member of Tatanka!

Everything that the Tatanka Lodge members did in their ceremonies came from Dr. Eastman's books plus a book written by Ernest Thompson Seton entitled *The book of Indian lore, and Woodcraft.* The books were written in the early nineteen hundreds.

Dr. Eastman was also instrumental in forming The Boy Scouts of America, and The Campfire Girls. Because of what they stand for, I call those two organizations the best "gangs" in America! All of his books immediately took the place of my Tarzan books! And, because at this writing I am eighty three years of age, I can truthfully say that for the rest of my life I have been deeply interested in Native America!

Now, I wanted to be like not only Tarzan, but also like the noble red man as well! In the books *The Soul of the Indian,* and *Indian Boyhood* by Dr. Eastman I learned some of what the true Lakota People believed in, and how they lived back in the old days.

I was given a book entitled *A Century of Dishonor*, written by Helen Kate Jackson. It told of the horrible injustices, and the many broken treaties perpetrated by the, at that time, young United States Government, on the American Indian Tribes.

At the library I came across a book about Indian sign language. It seems that when the first white settlers came to this continent, there were over 500 Indian tribes living here. Almost all of them spoke a different dialect, or an entirely different language than the other. Thru the centuries, the tribes had developed an intertribal hand sign language, that most tribes could understand.

They also devised a set of hand drawn symbols to represent certain things. In that book I discovered the Thunderbird! I do not pretend to be an Indian, but before I was twelve years old,

I had claimed the Thunderbird as my emblem! It's meaning is a combination of happiness and peace, and for some tribes the words "with honor" are added. At this writing, even after all these years, I still wear around my neck, a strip of deer thong. Attached to it is a solid gold medallion, with a thunderbird engraved upon it. There are many reasons why I have believed in it all my life.

Of course the deer thong has been replaced many times over. I still wear the medallion as proudly as I did when I was kid! Thats right! As one of my songs says, "The little boy in me just won't let go". I guess it never will!

Part 5: Growing Up

For the next nine years, eight weeks of my summers were spent at beautiful Camp Carson, in the Appalachian Mountains of Pennsylvania!

At the age of thirteen I became the youngest junior counselor in the history of the camp! At sixteen I became the youngest counselor! My job was to look after the twelve kids in my cabin.

Being in charge of the camp craft and woodlore department was my other job. I was teaching kids, not much younger than me, how to make fire without a match, how to find dry wood in the rain, and other wilderness survival skills. Most of those skills I was still in the process of learning myself!

I remember, as the years went by, each time I would come home after my eight weeks at camp, how hard it was to fall asleep at night in my house. After all those weeks breathing fresh air twenty-four hours a day, no matter how wide I opened my bedroom window at home, the air inside the house seemed stuffy and unhealthy to me. And altho there were some beautiful trees on the street that I lived, I really missed the forest in the mountains of Pennsylvania. It would take several weeks at home before I could adjust to "civilization".

At the age of seventeen I was really into wilderness survival. That same summer I became the youngest First War Chief, or president of Tatanka, ever! The lodge voted me first war chief again, the next summer! I also did something else for the first time! I picked up a guitar!

At night, after the kids were bedded down, and asleep, a lot of the counselors would go over to what we called "The Farm House". There we could write letters, converse grown up talk, and just relax. I would practice on my guitar. What a nuisance I must have been! I would go over the same chord, or the same line in a song, over and over again. Each chord took me a while to get all my fingers in the right place. One song might take me a half an hour to get thru. Although most of my friends would tell me how good I sounded, I'm quite sure that I was driving some of them nuts!

Part 6: Becoming a Pro With Snakes

When I turned twelve, I joined the JZSP! That's The Junior Zoological Society of Philadelphia! Every Saturday morning we would meet at the reptile house at the Philadelphia Zoo. I had to take three different trolly cars to get to the zoo from my home. I remember every Saturday morning during the winter, riding on a bridge over the Wissahicken Creek, seeing the forest below me, and wishing I could be down there in the woods, instead of on that trolly car.

One of the initial requirements for a prospective member of the JZSP is to give a four minute talk on a subject relating to zoology. Since I was so much into snakes, my speech was naturally on snakes. My topic was the long-nosed snake of Texas. Memorizing the only two paragraphs on the long-nosed snake in Roger Conant's book "What snake is that?" was easy. Giving the speech was not. It was the first time in my life that I had gotten up in front of people, to speak. I remember feeling weak, and my knees being wobbly, and once or twice momentarily losing my voice, but I managed to get thru it!

I enjoyed those Saturday morning meetings, and I made friends with young folks of a like mind. One of them I am still in touch with. His name is Sterling Williamson. He, like me, has retired now. For almost sixty years he had been a successful orthopedic surgeon!

The first snake book I bought was, and still is, a national treasure. It's a book entitled *Snakes of the World* by Raymond L. Ditmars. After that I bought or read everything I could get my hands on that dealt with snakes!

Several times a year the club would take a weekend field trip. One of the trips I remember the most was our weekend in the Pine Barrens of New Jersey. That's where I caught my first eastern hognose snake! It did all the tricks a good, respectable hognose snake should do! It played dead, and it acted like a cobra, but it didn't scare me!

What did scare me, but just for a moment, was my first real contact with a northern fence swift! That little lizard scampered out of my way, and jumped onto the trunk of a nearby tree. It looked like a tiny prehistoric monster hanging there! I knew about them, but I had never seen one. I went ahead and captured it, because one of my fellow members was into lizards, and I knew he would like to have it.

My second year as a member of the JZSP they voted me vice president of the club! My job was to help plan our field trips. Several times a year, during holidays the club would visit State Parks, wildlife refuges, and sometimes the uncharted areas that we would find on the Esso road maps. Back in those days there were still unmapped areas in Pennsylvania, New Jersey, and several other states. It was like exploring new territories, just as in the old frontier days!

I don't remember how old I was, but one fall, as always, school had started up again. My school was about two miles from my home, and I walked to and from it every day. On one of the streets along the way, there was a Presbyterian Church. Behind that church was a small graveyard. I had heard that there were snakes in that graveyard, and people were afraid of them.

Along the fence that bordered the graveyard there were a lot of stones lying flat on the ground. From the sidewalk I could reach thru the fence, and lift some of them. I decided that I was brave enough to try it, so one day I put my books down on the sidewalk, and got on my knees, and went to work!

It was amazing, but under the very first rock I lifted, I found a small harmless ring necked snake! Being so new at the game, I hesitated to grab it just long enough for it to slither away to safety! And it crawled under another stone further away! Now I couldn't reach it, because of the fence!

In just a few seconds I had experienced the thrill of both finding my quarry, and the disappointment of losing it! I would not be daunted! There were more rocks I could look under. And that is what I did. And eventually I began to catch snakes!

After a few harmless garter snake bites, I came to realize that the bite of nonvenomous snake is not painful, and seldom are there any after effects. Although their teeth are sharp they are tiny, and meant only to hold their victim. They cannot chew anything. The minute holes or scratches they might put on a person usually heal in a day or so. Of course in later years I learned to try to avoid being bitten, not for my sake, but for the sake of the snake. It might lose a tooth, and develop a disease known as mouth rot.

So now I was a young hopeful amateur herpetologist. I was catching my own snakes, and I was catching them right in the city streets of Philadelphia! Sometimes, if my homework would permit me the time, right after school I would run to the vacant lot I spoke of earlier, and lift everything I could find, trying to catch more snakes!

I was not allowed to keep them in the house. So they stayed in the garage. I built cages out of wood and screen to house them. In the first year or so of keeping snakes, I had numerous escapes to tend to. I finally learned how to build structures that were escape proof.

I'd keep a snake or for a couple of weeks, and turn it loose, back in the vacant lot where I caught it. None of the snakes I found in the Philadelphia area were venomous.

I remembered that at my elementary school, when I was really young, a man named Ross Allen visited our school with his snake show! He was great! He showed us a movie of him wrestling with a six foot alligator! And guess what? Thats right! Now I wanted to be like Ross Allen! He was a famous reptile handler in Silver Springs, Florida. And he bought snakes! Live ones! I wrote him a letter asking him how much he paid for them and how could I get them to him. He wrote back telling me, he would pay twenty-five cents a foot for copperheads, and I could ship them to him via railway express! He said I should make sure to label the box with, "Danger! Live poisonous snakes inside"! I found myself in the small time snake business.

I soon learned how to capture them without hurting them, or being hurt by them. On weekends in the spring I would hitch hike up to the mountains. I'd hunt snakes, and camp. I was young, I was growing up, and I was learning. All the way up until I joined the army, along with football, I camped, and hunted snakes in my spare time. I am sure there is a whole lot more I could say about the early days of my life, but I believe by now I've given enough answers to the question, Why snakes?

CHAPTER 10

"EARTH DAY EVERY DAY" WITH THE SNAKES

For over four decades in hundreds of schools of all grade levels, all over the Southeast, I delivered my *"Earth Day Every Day"* message. I wrote, sang and recorded songs praising all of *God's Creation*. And I always brought along a selection of live native venomous and nonvenomous snakes. They were not my pets. They were simply messengers, and truly excellent representatives of the natural world around us. They acted as my dynamic visual aids, and in most instances, during my presentation, they, themselves, taught the lessons. They helped my audiences to become "swampwise"!

Realizing that the greater part of my audience was in to, and accustomed to, watching TV or going to the movies, and that most of their knowledge of wild animals had come from the TV tube or the "make believe world" of the movie screen, I knew that "show and tell" would be my best bet to get my points across.

It is said that, "Seeing is believing," and my earthly, no shouldered ambassadors of good will animals would emphatically demonstrate that everything I was saying about them was true. And people would see it with their own eyes.

One of my methods was to place a large cottonmouth, a copperhead, and a rattlesnake, three very much alive, and extremely deadly and dangerous snakes, together on a small table, and slowly walk around the table.

As I walked, I talked. And as thoroughly as I possibly could, I would explain to my audience, what the snakes were teaching us.

First, I would bring out the fact that out there in the woods, under natural conditions, these snakes would never be seen together like that. They, like the American black bear, and many other wild animals, are solo creatures. Usually, the only time we would see them together would be during the mating season, or possibly in their winter quarters. But these three snakes were of different and separate species, and that copperhead would probably never be seen in the company of the other two. I was forcing them to disobey one of their rules of conduct![1]

I was walking around them so that everyone in my audience could see that the snakes were definitely aware of my presence. And that they were watching my every move.

The point I brought home is that the snakes definitely knew I was there, and yet they were not attacking me. They just stayed right where they were, on the table watching me. What they were showing us is that snakes, even venomous ones do not go out of their way to harm humans.

I had learned in the Okefenokee that wild animals of all breeds will attack with intent to kill only what they plan to eat. The rules of conduct for wild animals are plain and simple, yet harsh and exacting.

What it boiled down to is the simple fact that the snakes on the table did not know what I was, but they could see that I was much to big too eat! Therefore, the Golden Rule of Nature, *"If you don't need it, leave it!"*, would apply, and being members of the wild animal kingdom, they must obey. They would not bother or harm me in any way, unless I bothered them!

In this behavior on the part of the snakes, is a powerful lesson in tolerance toward humans. And because wild creatures never break Nature's Rules of Conduct, they show Strength of Character!

There are no snakes in the Okefenokee that grow big enough to eat a human. Their one and only reason for biting a human would be self-defense! And again, that comes under the heading of "fear"!

Then I mentioned the fact that the snakes were not bothering, or harming each other. And I would ask the question, "Are they all the same color, or the same breed?"

Naturally the audience would respond in unison, with a loud, "No!"

And again the simple, but powerful message in this case, is that wild animals, even those of different species, practice tolerance towards each other.

I added that, because they take only what they need, wild animals do not waste!

Their rules of conduct do not allow them to poison the earth, change the landscape, or kill because of ignorance!

These are just some of the lessons I, myself, was learning from our wild animal neighbors in the Okefenokee Swamp. And I was sharing as much as I possibly could with my fellow human beings, especially our young people.[2]

One by one, with my snake hook, I would carefully lift each snake up, and gently return it to its carrying box.

Before I opened the next box, I would calmly inform the audience that in the box was a large eastern diamondback rattlesnake. And I would say,

"It's the largest, and in my estimation, the most dangerous venomous snake in the United States of America! It is possibly the most dangerous in the world!"

Notice that I was saying, "most dangerous", not, "most deadly!" It's a toss-up between several species as to which snakes are the most deadly, the cobra family, the sea snakes, the kraits, the mambas, and other venomous snake varieties. The beautiful red, black, and yellow coral snake, being a member of the cobra family, is considered the most deadly snake found in our country. Drop for drop its venom is much more toxic than that of any of our other native species, including rattlesnakes. But to me, there is difference between the word *deadly* and the word *dangerous*.

A coral snake's reaction to capture or merely being restrained is usually to attempt escape. It seldom ever bites, or fights back in self- defense. An eastern diamondback rattlesnake is far more protective of itself, and it will bite anything that gets near it. I consider it to be not more deadly, but more dangerous than the others.

I would then pose the question, "Has anyone here ever heard of a mongoose?"

Some hands would go up, and I'd ask further,

"Has anyone here ever heard of a mongoose killing a cobra?"

A great many hands would go up in answer to that question. I would then add, "Have you ever wondered why there are no mongooses in America?"

I always allowed everyone to think about that for a moment. Some would begin to laugh.

I would then elaborate at great length. I would say,

"A mongoose would not stand a chance against a rattlesnake! Rattlers use an entirely different technique in striking. It's like the difference between *Kick Boxing,* and R*acket Ball!*

A cobra will rear up and spread its hood, and when it strikes it's in a downward motion, and much slower than that of a rattlesnake. The mongoose has no trouble getting up under the cobra before it can strike, and grabbing it by the head! Then it all but chews its head off, so it will never bite again. And then it swallows the snake!"

I would continue with,

"You see, the mongoose doesn't kill the snake because it hates it. The mongoose kills the snake because it loves it, just as we would love a bowl of vanilla ice cream. Along with that, if the mongoose isn't hungry, it'll walk right on by a snake. It simply and without question obeys the Golden Rule of Nature." *"If You Don't Need it Leave it!"*

I'd get back to my point with, "When a rattlesnake gets ready to strike, it doesn't do it like a sissy. It will coil, tighten every muscle in its body, and strike straight outward from its coil. Some rattlesnakes can reach a third of their body length! It is so fast that I doubt there is a wild animal or a human on earth that could dodge it, including a mongoose!"

By this time my enthusiastic audience would be on pins and

needles, in anticipation and ready to see the rattlesnake! They were more than prepared for the next lesson! I would then say,

"In a moment we are going to find out, with our own two eyes, where the only real danger is, when it comes to any of our native venomous snakes!"

I would move toward the box, put my hand on the handle of its lid, and excite my audience even more by saying, "Not to worry! You are perfectly safe anywhere in this room!" And I would add, "Except up here with me!"

Still holding the handle to the box lid, I'd step back a little and softly whisper, "Listen closely! I want you to hear what happens when I open the box!"

Naturally, as I slowly opened the box, the audience would hear silence! And I would quickly explain that the snake was already demonstrating two very important safety tips about rattlesnakes.

First of all, the moment I opened the box, it did not leap out, and try to hurt anyone. I'm quite certain that many of those watching were fully expecting that to happen, but it didn't. I mentioned the fact that it was demonstrating that looks can be deceiving. Snakes are incapable of changing their facial expression. And though, to some eyes, the snake looks evil it does not necessarily mean that it is evil. Everyone knows you can't judge a book by its cover.[3]

Secondly, it was teaching us what I consider to be the greatest danger for all humans! It was not rattling. And it was not rattling simply because it had not yet become aware of me. This is an important fact to know for our personal safety. If a snake doesn't know we are there, it would not know to rattle or to move out of our way! This is the greatest difference between snakes and all the other wild creatures. Most wild animals are highly alert, and will be long gone before we get close to them. Most snakes would not become aware of our approach until we are close enough to possibly step on one by mistake.

So the word is, since the snakes do not watch out for us, we must work twice as hard, and do the job for the snakes! We must be swampwise, and always remember to watch out for them!

I would ask,

"Can you imagine how a snake would feel if you stepped on it by mistake?"

I'd give everyone a little time to think about that, then I would say,

"Well it would hurt the snake! And it would have no way of knowing that you made a mistake! It would probably bite you!

Then I would lean over close to the open box, threatening the snake, and it would strike at me! It did not rattle when it did that, and it did not come all the way out of the box. Immediately after it struck, it pulled the forward part of its body back into the box, and remained coiled up safely inside it. Now it was rattling!

In just those few seconds two more very important lessons had been demonstrated.

The audience had seen just its head and a small portion of its body come out of the box when it struck at me, and they watched it immediately pull itself back into the box! In other words it carried the fight no further. Then it started to rattle. Everyone heard that! All were eye and ear witness to the fact that the deadly rattlesnake struck at me before it began to rattle.

We are fools and idiots to believe that rattlesnakes will always warn us before they bite. For our own safety we should toss that notion out the window![4]

By immediately retreating back into the relative safety of the box, it demonstrated that it had no plans to attack me!

Then, with my snake hook, I would carefully bring that huge and ferocious looking eastern diamondback rattlesnake out and gently place it on the table.

Rattling to beat the band, it would quickly coil in its defensive position. I would walk around it as I had done previously with the three other venomous snakes. The snake would turn completely around in its coils watching every move I was making. It did not strike at me; it just kept rattling and watching me. My purpose in doing that was to make sure that my audience knew that the snake knew I was there.

Then I would turn my back on the snake, and tell the story of how Skeeter, my tiny calico cat, had taught me long ago if a rattlesnake knows that you are near, it will not come near you. And you are safe as long as you do not get too close to the snake. And to prove that, for the next few minutes I would keep my back turned toward the snake.[5]

I would then tell the audience, "That rattlesnake knows I am here. Its bite could possibly kill me. But the snake doesn't know that. How could it? It does not even know what I am!"

"Do you see the size of its head? How big do you think the brain is in there? There is not much a snake, or any wild animal, for that matter, can fully understand. If it could think, which it can't, but if it could it would probably be wondering to itself",

"Jeepers! What is that big ugly white thing over there? That's the biggest rat I have ever seen in my life! If I have to bite that thing, where do I bite it? How much venom will it take to bring down something that big?"

And I would add.

"It does not know what I am, but it does know one thing about me. Don't you think it knows that I am too big to eat? That snake is afraid of me and it will not dare come near me. All wild animals, including snakes, strictly obey the Golden Rule of Nature! *"If you don't need it, leave it!"*

And until the end of the demonstration it would prove that everything I was saying about it was true!

With that dangerous snake watching every move I was making, I'd go on elaborating on its attitude and behavior toward humans. I would say,

"It's showing us that it will not attack something too big to eat, but at the same time it is showing us something else thats important to understand. Its standing its ground! It will not run away!

Through experience, I had learned that if a Diamondback is in strange territory and not sure where the nearest safe haven is, invariably it will choose to stand its ground and face its intruder no matter what the odds. I've seen wild ones stop right in the middle of a dirt road, coil up and face an oncoming pickup truck. It doesn't do the snake any good, but such is its nature. If it is not sure it can escape, it will elect to stand its ground and fight to the death! It is not going to run, and it is not going to attack!

After about ten minutes, all who were watching the show had seen, with their own two eyes, the true attitude and behavior of a rattlesnake, the most dangerous snake in our country, toward a human. They not only saw it, they actually experienced it. And as the saying goes, experience is the best teacher. And it was an experience that most of them will never forget as long as they live![6]

As I spoke, the rattlesnake would remain at bay, watching me. Finally, during the last part of my presentation, I would move close to the snake, raise my arms and act as if I was going to attack it! I always made sure that I was far enough away from it, so that it could not reach me, but close enough to make it strike at me. And it would then strike at me!

In the one split second it took to strike at me, it proved that it would bite a human only in self-defense. It also demonstrated how far it could actually reach! And I would jokingly make mention of the fact that, "Some people think they can jump clean across the highway!"

That usually got a laugh from my audience, and I would add,

"*Thank God* there is no such thing as Super Snake!"

That got a better laugh!

Throughout my entire presentation, the snakes, acting as nature's ambassadors of good will, had been demonstrating the most important lesson of all. It's a lesson that the entire human race, all across the world should be aware of, and act accordingly.

The lesson? Well, we had all seen with our own two eyes that *there definitely are ways for the human race to safely coexist with all of God's Creations in the natural world, including venomous snakes!* And I would then end my presentation by adding the question,

"But guess who needs to learn the rules?"

"Swampwise"

Notes:

[1] The rules of conduct for wild animals are exacting, and at times extremely harsh. And under natural conditions, no wild animal in the swamp will break those rules! See Chapter 12!

[2] Every Monday was my day to take the park truck, and drive up town to pick up supplies for the park. I had a made a deal with the grocery stores, and the fish markets, that I could have some of the fresh vegetables, meats, and other products that they didn't sell over the weekend, to feed my animals. I would tell people in town that I was learning a lot from our wild animal neighbors, and I suppose the people up town thought I was crazy, but it's true!

[3] Nature does not care if we like snakes or not. Nature needs its snakes. It needs all of them, venomous included. That is what I came to realize in the Okefenokee Swamp, and that is why I did what I did, day after day. The best thing we humans can do is to learn more about the snakes than just to be afraid of them. See my book "Snake Hunter Snake Talk".

[4] Rattlesnakes in particular, spend a great deal of their entire lifetime sleeping. On any given day, if the temperature is right, some snakes will come out of their safe hiding place. Some may look for another rodent burrow, because they are hungry. Some may come out to find water, or to bask in the sun to help prepare their skin for the shedding process. And some may come out because, "Hey man, it feels good out here!" Those will be the most dangerous for us that day. In a short while they will be lying coiled up and sound sleep somewhere! A sleeping snake would not know to move out of your way, and if you are not looking out, you may step on or too close to it, and be bitten!

[5] It was my tiny calico cat Skeeter that showed me for the first time that a snake will attack only what it plans to eat, and we are safe as long as we do not get near the snake! More detail about that in chapter 3 of this writing, "Skeeter the cat"'

[6] I know that because, for four wonderful decades I appeared at county fairs, Indian pow-wows, sportsman's shows, schools, libraries, and museums. Often I was in front of over a million people on television. Everywhere I went dozens of people would come up to me, shake my hand and tell me how much they appreciated what I was doing! I can honestly say that I was doing what *God* wanted me to do. And what a wonderful and rewarding experience my life has been!

CHAPTER 11

OKEFENOKEE JOE'S SWAMPWISE SNAKE SAFETY TIPS

First and most importantly, I am not, never will be, nor will I ever claim to be an expert on the subject of snakes! I am the first to admit that I am an amateur herpetologist which means I do not have a degree in herpetology, and my layman's knowledge of reptiles has not come from books, or schools of higher learning. It has come from many years of hands on experience in both hunting them, and keeping them in captivity.

That is why I do not consider myself to be an expert. How could I be? I keep learning more every day. It is both exciting, and exhilarating. I hope it never ceases to be so! That being said, here are <u>my best snake safety hints</u>, and they are coming to you from the half a century experience and the knowledge of a really *swampwise* snake hunter:

1. Most snakes do not stay very long in damp places. Even the aquatic minded species spend most of their time in a high and dry habitat.
2. Snakes do not hibernate. Not in the true sense of the word. On warm days in the winter they sometimes will be found lying outside their winter quarters, ready to go back in when the temperature drops.

"Swampwise"

3. The greatest danger involving venomous snakes is that, unlike most furry creatures, a snake might not become aware of your approach, and move out of your way, and if you are not watching out you might step on it.
4. Snakes have no ears. Noise will not scare them away. They may feel vibration in the ground, but never count on that fact to chase a snake away! Use your eyes!
5. Certain species crawl at night, and certain others crawl in the day time. It's best to use a flashlight at night.
6. Always be aware of where you are putting your hands, your feet, or any part of your body!
7. The saying "If you leave a snake alone, it will leave you alone!" is true. That goes for the venomous species too!
8. Do not believe everything you read about snakes in magazines or newspapers. The same applies to what you might see about snakes in the movies, or on TV.
9. When you see a snake of any kind, your best bet is to remember the Golden Rule of Nature, "If you don't need it, leave it!"
10. A comforting fact about venomous snakebites is that out of possibly hundreds of snake bite cases in the US each year, only seven or eight end in death!
11. Another comforting fact: In forty percent of venomous snake bite cases in the US, no venom was injected. It's called a "dry bite"!
12. In the event of snakebite, if nothing serious occurs within the first half hour after the bite, it usually means that the victim's system is keeping the venom at bay temporarily. It's time to get to the hospital!
13. In the event of snakebite, do not waste precious time cutting, and sucking near the bite area. It's been proven that it's best to just apply a loose tourniquet above the bite area, and get the victim to the hospital!
14. When snakes are in the process of shedding their skin, their vision is somewhat impaired, but they are by no means blind. Nor are they any weaker.

15. Although all snakes are capable of climbing trees, and swimming in the water. Most snakes seldom do either one.
16. A young venomous snake's venom may or may not be more toxic than an adult. They are both exceedingly dangerous!
17. All of *God's Creation*, including the snake, has been placed here on earth help maintain the balance. Snakes would not be around if they were not necessary to *God's natural scheme of things*.
18. Learn how to identify the four venomous snakes of the United States. Never again will you need to ask, "How can you tell if it poisonous?"
19. Snakes shed their skin periodically throughout the year. Not necessarily during "Dog Days".
20. We can identify snakes by examining their shed skins. If you find a snake shed, whichever way the tail is pointing, that's the direction the snake went.
21. Any snake can bite under water, including the dreaded cottonmouth.
22. The cottonmouth does not live in water. It lives on land, and it breathes the same air we do. It merely lives near water, because most of its food items live in the water.
23. If you find one snake, it does not necessarily mean there must be another close by.
24. The only time a rattlesnake will rattle is when it is wide awake, it realizes danger is near, and it is not sure it can escape. It is fear that makes it rattle! And that fear is the only reason it would bite you!
25. Although anything is possible, it is highly unlikely that a snake would crawl into your sleeping bag while you are sleeping in it.
26. There is no such thing as a "pilot snake". No snake needs another snake to show it the way.
27. The cottonmouth received its name because the tissue and the fang sheaths in its mouth appear to be white and fluffy.

28. Nature needs snakes, and does not care if humans like them or not. Our safest bet is to learn about them.
29. There is no poison or harmful dust in the rattles of a rattlesnake.
30. A snake will attack only what it plans to eat. And it does know we humans are too big to eat!
31. If a snake is seen on a paved road at night it is just passing through. It was not attracted to the road because of its warmth, and it never curls up, and falls asleep on the road.
32. A snake would bite a cold boot stepping on it, for the same reason it would bite a warm hand reaching for it. FEAR!
33. Snakes do not mean to frighten you. Snakes have more important things to do!
34. Snakes eat rats, not people!
35. Don't stand still when you see a snake, like they do in the movies. Move away from it. But look around you first, and be careful not to step on another one.
36. In the event of snakebite do not let the snake bite again! Its first bite might be a dry bite, and would have no ill effect. But if it has reason to bite again it will have had time to program itself to give its victim a lethal dose! The only reason it would bite a second time would be if your foot is still on it, or you are still holding it.
37. Do not allow piles of tin, lumber or trash to accumulate near your home. It makes wonderful "man-made habitat" for snakes, and other creatures like rats and mice, or black widow spiders!
38. No matter how much venom a snake has recently used to bite and kill a rat, it will always keep enough to possibly constitute a lethal dose for a human!
39. A diamond shaped head is not a perfect method of identifying a venomous snake.
40. The tongue of a snake is a sense organ that aids in its sense of smell. The snake would probably not survive without it.

41. We cannot tell if a snake is venomous by the color of its tongue.
42. Snakes can see very well in the dark.
43. Very few snakes on earth are capable of digging their own burrow.
44. Snakes, just like people come in different color phases. That's why it is sometimes very difficult to match a snake up with a picture in the encyclopedia.
45. If you do not have time, or are in the habit of forgetting to watch where you put your feet, wear boots!
46. We recognize four types of venomous snakes native the US. That's not many to remember. Learn them!
47. Three of the four types of native venomous snakes, the copperhead, the cottonmouth, and the rattlesnake are pit vipers. Called such because midway between its eyes and its nose, on either side of its face, is a deep pit. It senses heat!
48. The eyes our three native pit vipers are vertically elliptical. Their eyeballs look like slits straight up and down in the middle of each eye.
49. Our native venomous coral snake has a black nose. It's beautiful and bright red, black, and yellow bands encircle its entire body. Its belly is just as striking as its back. A bright narrow yellow band separates every band on its body.
50. While you are driving, and you should see a snake crossing the road, please do not run over it! Remember "Nature needs her snakes!"
51. Most importantly, (A few repeats) always watch where you are placing your hands or your feet. If you see a snake of any kind, remember the Golden Rule of Nature: "If you don't need it, leave it!" You, the snake, Mother Nature, and the earth, all things will be better off if you do that!

CHAPTER 12
NATURE'S RULES OF CONDUCT

Part 1: The Golden Rule of Nature

All of the animals and plants in my care, and all of the wild ones close around me in the Okefenokee were constantly teaching me lessons. I became more "swampwise" every day! Much of what I was learning has never been written in a book. As a matter of fact, many of the animal behavior patterns I was witnessing totally disagreed with my book learning. I attribute that to the fact that my education was now coming to me directly from the plants and animals themselves. And what a golden opportunity it was!

Early on I was discovering that each and every rule or natural law I was being taught, was faithfully and devotedly followed by every single living thing in the swamp! And under natural conditions none of them will ever break those laws. I call them simply "Nature's Rules of Conduct."[1]

I consider one the rules in particular to be by far the most important wildlife lesson that I have learned, or ever will learn, in my entire life! It explains in a nutshell, what many college courses will take months, and even years to cover! It is my belief that the entire human race should be aware of it, and do its best to abide by it! I call it simply *"The Golden Rule of Nature"!*

Any wild animal could teach us that rule. A redtail hawk could do it. So could a Virginia whitetail deer. But those animals are extremely difficult to keep up with out in the forest. We'd soon lose sight of them, and we'd never know where they went or what they were up to.

When I tell people which animal taught me the *"Golden Rule of Nature"* for the very first time, some people laugh, but it's absolutely true.

A tiny ant taught me. That's right! Even an insignificant pest of an insect can teach us lessons.

One afternoon while I was sitting on our "Cypress Stump" waiting for my bobcat friend Streak to show up there, I found myself watching a red ant as it moved across the ground around my feet. I noticed how it would touch, and thoroughly investigate everything it came to. Obviously it was busy searching for something.

Several times, without disturbing it, the ant climbed up and down a single blade of grass. It went under one side of a piece of pine bark, and came out on the other side without moving or disturbing the bark. Coming across a rather large brown grasshopper, it backed off, and the grasshopper did the same. They left each other alone and went their separate ways.

It checked out leaves, twigs, and just about everything in sight. Sometimes it circled back to where it had been before and studied the same things over again, not harming or changing anything, just investigating.

I had to get up from my seat on the stump to follow it further. Finally, the ant came across a caterpillar. It was wiggling, and acting as if it was wounded and in pain. This must have been what the ant was looking for, because, without hesitation it quickly seized the caterpillar in its mandible! Then it proceeded to drag it away. It was an amazing feat of strength on the ant's part, because that caterpillar was nine or ten times its size, and it was struggling to escape.

The ant was determined to hold on at all costs. Apparently it was carrying it back to the nest, for all the ants in the colony to enjoy.

By now Streak the bobcat had arrived at our meeting place,

and I had to leave ant watching because Streak needed our daily 'pet and purr' time, and so did I!

I found my ant observation to be extremely interesting, and enlightening, and for me, it opened the door to the beginning of my understanding, and interpretation of "The Golden Rule of Nature".

In those brief five minutes of 'ant watching', I had learned that, ants will allow nothing to stand in the way of their task at hand. No matter what the circumstances, ants will stay focused. They do not take or try to change anything until they find what they are looking for. In most cases that would be food. They do not play with, tease or harm anything they do not need! Simply put, ants are not one bit wasteful! Not even with their time!

Plants and trees also demonstrate the Golden Rule of Nature! Everyone knows that a tree or a blade of grass will take from the earth, the sun, and the rain only what it needs, and nothing more! Like the ants, the plants of *God*'s earth are not one bit wasteful.

Every wild animal I was working with demonstrated the same attitude and behavior as the ant had shown me. My experiences with all the wild animals including, the bears, the bobcat, the alligator, the river otter, the snakes, the birds of prey, and others, undeniably back up the knowledge I first gained from that tiny ant. I was realizing more than ever that although "Streetwise" is cool; "Swampwise" is awesome"!

With my own eyes I have witnessed huge, tough, and ferocious American black bears jump away from, and avoid contact with animals like snakes! Most snakes are capable of moving extremely fast when trouble comes their way. Bears can move fast too. As a matter of fact a bear can outrun a deer. But it seldom does that partly for the same reason it will not chase a snake.

Bears take life slow and easy. Although a bear will sometimes stalk its prey, it very apparently does not care to go through the exertion of running to catch its food.

Besides that, a bear is an omnivore. It eats anything that's edible. Because of the abundance of plant life in the swamp, bears have no need to work hard to 'make a living'.

Wherever it happens to be, if it feels hunger coming on, a

black bear can simply roll over on its back, pull up a plant, roots and all, and blissfully 'munch out'! No, bears will not go to the trouble of chasing a snake!

I found another definitive example of this behavior with the Virginia whitetail deer. I was caring for eleven of them in our exhibit, and I was surrounded by hundreds of them in the great Okefenokee Swamp! I was with my captive deer often, observing them and learning from them. On many occasions, I've seen a deer react to the sight of a snake the same way a bear would do. They just ignore them and go their separate ways. Once I witnessed a deer actually jump back and run from a harmless black racer!

Of course, as everyone knows, deer do not eat meat. Deer are herbivores, and therefore they consume only plant life. They have no need for snakes, and just like the bear, they too leave them alone.[2]

On the other hand, none of the snakes of the Okefenokee grow large enough to consume a bear or a deer. And any wild animal, including a snake, will do its utmost to avoid contact with another wild animal that is too big to eat.[3]

Under natural conditions, if these animals encounter one another, they do something so amazingly wonderful! Something all of us could learn from! They simply mind their own business! And in doing so they demonstrate that there is no such thing as hate among wild animals! Could we learn from that?

They do not even get close to each other! Just as the ant had shown me, they do not waste their time bothering, changing, or harming anything they do not need.[4]

And although the word humane does not exist in the vocabulary of a wild animal, if a kill is made it is done quickly, with little or no suffering on the part of the victim![5]

The "Golden Rule of Nature" is central to the cycle of all life on earth! And yet, it is so remarkably simple that even a small child could understand it! I believe that all humans should learn of it, and abide by it. The world would be a better place if that were to happen!

It explains the basic technology of the earth that we live upon! It's the very reason life on earth can exist! Without it we humans could not breath the air, drink the water, or grow food in the soil.

The combined efforts of billions and billions of life forms in the natural world, each minding its own business, working at the job it's been created to do, and taking only what it needs, that makes it work![6]

The Golden rule of Nature is what made the earth like it is, and keeps it like it is, so that we humans can live upon it! It's a plan created centuries ago by a power far greater, far more intelligent, and far more important than the entire human race put together!

It's only seven humble and simple words, yet it speaks mountains and oceans of wisdom, and understanding, and here it is!

"If You Don't Need It Leave it!"

If it is not something you can use, don't bother it, don't touch it, don't harm it, & don't molest it, don't tease it, just leave it!

Notes:

[1] Nature's Rules of Conduct govern the life of all living things in the swamp!
[2] I was beginning to understand that since wild animals avoid and do no harm to things they do not need, possibly there is no such thing as hate among wild animals!
[3] The ancient law of the jungle is "If I am bigger than you I eat you!" Upon seeing another wild animal that is much too big to eat, all animals will immediately realize that the creature is also big enough to eat them.
[4] Each and every one of the rules of conduct for wild animals sets an example, and teaches an important and valuable lesson for humans to follow. We could learn a lot from the attitudes displayed by our 'Wild animal neighbors', if we'd just look up, and pay attention! The world just might be a better place if we did that!

[5] The cat family is the one and only exception to that rule. Many members of the cat family, including, and especially domestic cats, will play with, or better said, torture their prey until it finally dies. It's sad but true.

[6] Every living plant and animal on this earth has been designed perfectly by the creator, to do the particular job it has been created to do. And "if they don't need it, they leave it!"

Part 2: Fear versus Anger

After several years of living in the swamp, working with the animals under my care, and observing the ones in the wild, I had begun to realize that many of the things about them that I had learned from a book, or seen in the movies, were not entirely accurate. For example, I spent the better part of eighteen months working on what I called 'The Black Bear Project'.

As often as I possibly could I was out in the back of the park, recording the sounds that my captive American black bears would make. And there are many! I managed to photograph them demonstrating the mood they were in, as they made each particular sound. By studying the picture as I listened to the tape recording, I was able to fairly, and I believe accurately, interpret what each bear was saying.

I learned that bears do not just make meaningless bear sounds. There actually is a definite meaning to each sound that we hear them make. I am quite positive of that.

The project was time consuming, extremely interesting, and greatly rewarding. I was learning a lot about bears from the bears themselves.

Because of our fascination with animals, we humans often think of them as having the same feelings that we do. Walt Disney took advantage of that idea, and made a fortune with his animal cartoons, and films filled with anthropomorphism.

And yet, in reality, animals, especially the wild ones are actually not capable of comprehending most things the way we humans can. They cannot think as we think, and therefore they sometimes do not act or react in life situations the way we would expect them to do. And we often make the mistake of trying to interpret in them the same feelings as ours. And that is impossible! They do not possess the brain power to comprehend much more beyond survival. I was learning from my bears, and other animals that it is up to us to do the understanding. I believe the bible tells us the same thing!

I did a special half hour documentary for the local TV station in Waycross, Georgia, interpreting what my bears would say to each other. We would show a picture of a bear on the screen, and play the sound it was making at the time the picture was taken. And I would tell the audience what I thought the bear was saying. It was really a very interesting half hour documentary. It received quite a bit of attention. I still have a copy of it in my file somewhere.

One extremely interesting, but slightly disappointing fact I learned from my 'Bear Project', is that of the many different sounds bears make, I was able to translate only two meanings. In other words I was learning that, unlike humans, there are only two emotions that bears are capable of displaying, and therefore feeling!

I wondered to myself,

"Is that possible? Bears comprehend only two things in their entire lifetime?"

One is fear! Or one of the many forms of fear such as being uptight, unsure, confused, protective, and all of the aspects or emotions related to fear.

The other is desire! Such as wanting or needing something, and all the aspects, or emotions connected with desire.

I have seen living proof of this over and over again in other wild animals, including hundreds of snakes, and insects of all kinds. It is my belief that in the mind of a wild animal anger, jealousy, hate, greed, envy, other such undesirable human emotions simply do not exist. I believe that those emotional problems exist only in the mind of human beings. And I can cite many examples to back up my theory.

For example, when some people hear the sound of a rattlesnake rattling its rattles, they often assume that the snake is angry. I'll admit that, to the ears of a human, the very sound of the rattle could be associated with anger, but in my lifetime I have dealt with hundreds of rattlesnakes, and this is my assumption to that assumption. Again, first a question:

If a rattlesnake shakes its tail and rattles because it is angry, why does it never attack its intruder?

I've never seen one attack me! Naturally should a person get to close to the snake, and become a real threat, most certainly it will strike in self-defense. But immediately after it strikes it will always go back into its defensive coiled up and rattling position. The only thing I have ever seen a rattlesnake actually go out of its way to attack is a rabbit, or something it plans to eat!

But because it is a hunter, in those cases it never rattles! The sound of the rattles would alert its prey of its presence, and the intended victim would probably escape!

I have never seen a snake of any kind, venomous or not attack me. I've teased them, poked at them with a stick, and gone to all sorts of drastic measures to make them angry at me. Rattlesnakes will defend themselves to the death, but they simply will not attack anything that is too big to eat! Even when molested they will fight back, but never will they attack!

I say it is fear, and fear alone that causes a snake to vibrate its tail!

Corner or confuse a harmless black snake, or a King Snake, or almost any snake, and if it feels that it can't get away from you, it will vibrate its tail just like a rattlesnake. Again, it is fear that makes a snake of any kind, including a rattlesnake, vibrate its tail.

That fear is the reason, and the only reason a snake would have for biting something as large as a human. Not anger, not malice or revenge, but fear!

By the end of four decades, in 2014, I had been in front of millions of people with my *Earth Day Every Day* presentations all through the Southeast. I had appeared before more millions of people on Television, and YouTube! In every single snake presentation I had allowed a live and extremely dangerous, eastern diamondback rattlesnake to effectively demonstrate that fact! I often made the statement that,

"It was about time someone told the snake's side of the story, and told the truth!"

In all those years I not only told the truth, I allowed the snakes themselves to show the truth!

In my following observations of the "American alligator" lies further proof of fear vs anger in a wild animal.

It is common knowledge that out in the swamp, a big bull alligator will choose its own territory. It may be just a few yards, or a few hundred yards, but it will belong to him. It will guard and patrol its territory night and day. And the bull gator shows a great deal of tolerance, because it will allow almost every wild animal living in the swamp into its realm. All the female alligators are most certainly welcome. All the birds, all the fish, turtles, snakes, deer, and small furry creatures can come in. He might be able to catch one someday, and make a meal of it. The bull gator will welcome all living things into its territory. Except for one!

Anyone could probably guess what would happen if the big bull gator found another bull gator in its territory!

Yes they are going to fight! And it can be terrible painful and bloody struggle for both of them. One might lose an eye or a leg, or part of its tail, or even part of its jaw. But the astonishing thing to me is the fact that I have never seen the battle end in death! The weaker one, the one that loses is allowed to swim away. If death should occur, I'd be willing to bet, it was not intentional.

In a few weeks or months, or however long it takes for its wounds to heal, the rogue gator will invariably try to sneak back in. The big bull gator will soon become aware of its presence, and there will be another bloody battle. But again the fight will not end in death for either of them. Why not? I was being shown over and over again that any battle between animals of the same species is not caused by anger, jealousy, envy, greed, or hate, as in humans!

Another example is in the attitude and behavior of male deer during mating season. Many a deer hunter has seen male deer, during the rutting season lock antlers, and fight over mating rights. It can be a terrific battle, and it will rage on sometimes more than an hour, until one of the deer gives up. It too, just like the losing bull gator, is allowed to walk away. Battles between deer over mating rights seldom ever end in death.

Wolves teach the same lesson! I was told once by a man who kept wolves, and did educational shows about them at sporting events, that if a young male wolf challenges the leader of the pack, naturally they will fight. Each one of them will end up a bloody mess. But the loser is allowed to walk away from the fight. And again, if death does occur it was most certainly not intentional on the part of either combatant.

Further, if the wolf that loses stays with the pack, it will be shunned by all the other members. For as long as it stays with the pack it will be the last to get to the food, the last one to mate with another wolf, the last in line for every aspect of pack life among the wolves.

Such is the way of the natural world around us. I was learning that battles between animals, especially of the same species, are never fought over the same things humans fight over. I do not believe that the emotions mentioned above, such as anger, jealousy, envy, greed, or hate exist in the mind of a wild animal. That is one of the reasons we humans so often misinterpret the actions of wild animals.

On that same subject, here is yet another example of fear vs anger in wild animals.

We often hear it said that if a hunter were to shoot and wound a black bear, that the bear would get mad at him, and attack him. I would agree that if we wound a bear, yes it might come after us. But I firmly disagree that its motivation would be anger, and I would ask the question,

"If someone were to shoot you with a gun, and wound you, do you think at that moment you'd be mad at that person, or would you be shocked, in terrible pain, and just possibly somewhat frightened almost out of your wits?

When the time came to put the bears on exhibit in their natural

"Swampwise"

habitat compound at the park, we put Black Jack, our biggest bear, in first. We had constructed an electric fence, hidden from view of the public, hoping it would keep the bears up closer to the viewing area. Not knowing what to expect of him, I watched him closely, especially during his first few hours in his new surroundings.

At first we had a problem keeping him in sight of our visitors. We soon solved that by redoing the electric fence. After that, though it took several weeks, Black Jack seemed to settle in. He knew where he could, and couldn't go. And he stayed in view of the public.

When it was decided that Black Jack was fully accustomed to and comfortable in his new home, we introduced the second bear into the compound.

It was a much smaller female bear named June. Both bears had been kept separate from one another, and I imagine that neither one, in their lifetime had ever come in physical contact with another bear.

Before little June had had a chance to investigate her new surroundings, she spotted Black Jack. The mere sight of that huge male bear must have horrified her, because, with all caution aside, and loudly, almost screaming her "yeng, yeng, yeng" bear cry of distress she ran from him. In her blind panic, running around the compound, what was bound to happen, did happen! She hit the electric fence! She had not even seen it!

It not only shocked her, it terrified her! And in an instant she turned and ran straight at Black Jack!

Black Jack had been standing up on his hind legs watching her, and because of her rapid momentum, when she hit him it knocked him completely off his feet!

In a second, still in a panic, June was running away from Black Jack, back toward the fence, and she hit it again!

Immediately she bounced off the fence, and again ran straight at Black Jack! This time he was on all fours, and when she hit him, it didn't knock him down. It just surprised him!

Immediately after hitting Black Jack that second time, still in utter panic, and screaming her "yeng, yeng, yeng" she ran back toward the fence, and, for the third time hit it again!

This time she did not attack Black Jack. In desperation she ran to a corner of the compound, as far away from him, and the fence as she could get! And she just stood there, whimpering, and shaking her head back and forth, sideways! Poor little June was totally frightened, frustrated, confused, and completely out of control!

What I had just witnessed was caused not by anger, but by pure, raw, mortal pain and fear! It was obvious that June was frightened by the mere sight of Black Jack. And because of her fear she blindly ran from him. She was then taken by sudden and complete surprise, when she felt the shock from the electric fence.

Apparently she connected the fear and the pain from touching the fence, with the same fear she felt at the sight of Black Jack. In her confused and bewildered state of mind she fought back by attacking Black Jack! Fear and fear alone is what motivated June's every confused reaction in that rapidly unfolding, and confusing situation!

So, back to the hunter wounding a bear, if the wounded bear does attack the hunter, it is my belief that the attack would have been caused by fear, not because of anger.

Further, I do not believe the word anger is in the mind or the vocabulary of any living thing in the natural world. And for now, I rest my case on Fear versus Anger!

Part 3: Revenge? No SuchThing!

One spring a wild American black bear began raiding the park at night, dumping trash cans, and making a mess in general all around the main park area. The mess had to be cleaned up each morning, before visitors began to arrive. So the bear was a nuisance, and had to be removed.

"Swampwise"

From the Georgia State Game Commission, we borrowed a live trap that had been mounted on wheels for easy transport. One night at quitting time, I set the trap out in back of the park, using one of the black bear's most tempting treats for bait! It was a pack of sugar coated donuts dipped in honey! I even poured a short trail of honey leading to the open door of the trap. I said a short prayer, and left for the night.

The next morning, sure enough, we had caught the culprit in the trap. It was a pretty good size for a swamp black bear. It was every bit of three hundred pounds! When it saw me approaching, it let out with its "yeng, yeng, yeng" black bear sound of fear, and alarm! It slammed its body violently against the sides of the trap, trying to break out! It had not been harmed by the trap, it just wanted out! Thank goodness the trap was made to withstand such harsh punishment!

We called the Game Commission, and one of the wardens came out to haul the bear away. I had been given permission to ride with him. We hooked the trailer to his truck, and drove off.

The game warden had been given orders to turn the bear loose on the far side of the swamp, near Fargo, Georgia. And that is where we went. The bear seemed pretty quiet as we rode along. It only gave out with that "yeng, yeng, yeng" sound when we'd stop at a traffic light or for some other reason. We reached our destination, and backed the trailer up to the spot where we planned to turn the bear loose.

Neither of us were sure what the bear would do the moment the door to the trap was opened, and it would be allowed to escape. I whispered a short prayer to *God*, and we both climbed up on top of the trap, and pulled it open!

Immediately that bear jumped out of the trap, without sparing a second to look back, it "hightailed it" into the woods and was gone! We never saw it again!

Obviously it never crossed its mind to hang around and get even, or to take revenge upon its captors. It simply wanted gone! All it wanted was to be left alone, to just be a black bear doing what black bears are supposed to do, out there in the woods!

The snakes we would catch and later release did the same as the big black bear had done. They simply crawled away as quickly as they could, to get away from us. They never once looked back!

For over four decades in my *Earth Day Every Day* snake safety demonstration I allowed the most dangerous venomous snake in America to set an example for all wild animals! Over and over again it would prove beyond a doubt that the only way it would bite a human is in self-defense! Not because of anger, or revenge, or any other supposed reason. Only in self-defense, and out of fear!

If we mistakenly step on a fire ant bed, when the ants bite us they are not seeking revenge. They are merely trying to protect their homes by driving us away!

Mosquitoes and other biting insects do not bite us out of anger. They bite us because of hunger.

Bees or wasps do not sting us because they are angry with us. They do it to protect themselves or their homes by driving us away the same as the ants will do. I have never seen any wild animal in the swamp in anger or seeking revenge. The word, and the meaning of it, is simply not in the vocabulary of a wild animal. And neither are all the rest of the unpleasant feelings or attitudes we humans so often display. Just as we humans all wild animals are created by *God our Father Almighty,* and they, unlike humans, will simply not disobey their *"Rules of conduct"*

All wild animals, and all wild plants are swampwise! Could we learn from that?

CHAPTER 13
MOVIN' ON

At the time of this writing, the swampwise lessons for me are not yet over. I pray to *God* that they never will be over. I love being swampwise! And learning more, always!

Thus far the teachings I have been given from the plants and animals themselves, have shown me that when *God* created each animal or plant he instilled in it first of all a definite job to perform for the balance of all the nature he had created on his earth. And he designed each form of life perfectly so that it would be able to easily perform that job.

I can also see that his complicated but perfect life systems intertwine so beautifully, and harmoniously in every way that it could not possibly just evolved that way. It's all too perfect! It is too well-planned. I need no further proof or truth to believe that *God, our father almighty* does certainly exist, and is alive today, and that he, and he alone did all the creating! It didn't just happen! I believe that the "Big Bang Theory" is a hoax!

And everything, from the tiniest microscopic plant, animal or stone to the greatest tree, whale, or mountain, everything on earth plays an active and necessary role in the scheme of things. For that reason all things on earth are connected! It also means that all things are necessary! All things that is, except for possibly one, and that is you and me, the human race!

The *Bible* tells us that we are to "have dominion over the earth," which, to me and people like me, means that we are to be Keepers of the Earth. In other words, just as a shepherd tends his flock, we should be caring for the earth, and all things upon it. In that respect, just maybe, we humans could be connected to the system.

I believe that possibly there is one other way that we could be connected, and play a role in the system. As mentioned earlier, according to the bible we humans are the last form of life to be created. We are also the only living things on this planet that have been blessed with a brain that is capable of feelings and truly deep understandings far beyond the reach of any plant or animal in the natural world. Instilled within our brain are the power and the ability to understand and appreciate all manner and facets of life on this planet. We have been given that ability, and I, for one, believe we've also been given the responsibility to do that.

Maybe that's another of *God*'s reasons why we are here! Maybe that's also why we humans were the last thing to arrive on earth! After *God* had created such a wonderful world full of life and beauty, he wanted something on this earth that could understand, and appreciate all that he had done!

Bears can't do it. A blade of grass or a tree can't do it. The clouds, the sun, the moon, the stars cannot do it. The only living thing on earth that is capable of doing the understanding, the only living thing that can do the appreciating is you, and me! We human beings!

Just as I was the only living thing in the Okefenokee Swamp that wasn't necessary or needed in the scheme of things, the entire human race is merely a guest on this planet! And as such we should all be grateful, and act accordingly.

God also instilled in every animal the following traits, and characteristics that most decent humans on this earth prefer to, and strive to abide by all their lives. It truly amazed me to learn this!

Showing strength of character, each and every wild plant and animal in the swamp is totally willing and devoted to cooperate with, and obey *The Golden Rule of Nature, "If You Don't Need it, Leave it!"* They do not waste. Not even their time! They never neglect their responsibilities. All of them are good, cooperative team members, and do their jobs willingly, without question or hesitation. Each and every one of them practice extreme patience, and are tolerant of one another. They are self-sufficient. They do not hold a grudge, or take revenge. And they do not kill because of ignorance, anger, jealousy, envy, hate, greed, or lust!

In essence, all wildlife in the swamp demonstrates its willingness to obey, or to cooperate with one of the most important rules that *God* has given man to obey! And it came to us through the words of *Jesus Christ* over two thousand years ago! The rule is simply *"Forgiveness!"*

It is amazing that they display all these attributes without being able to read a book or converse at any great length with each other. Equally amazing is the fact that they do not need a police force to make them obey the rules. They just do it!

We humans have been both blessed, and at the same time cursed with this brain of ours!

The *Bible* says, "No man is without sin". In order to get along with each other we so often must fight off feelings such as anger, jealousy, envy, greed, and hate! Those are all human faults, and human problems! Wild animals do not have those problems. Could we learn from that?

Life in the Okefenokee Swamp was beautiful. I was living so close the earth, and in such a clean, healthy, and quiet environment! I often took the time to sit on the steps of my front porch, and reflect on all the swampwise wisdom that seemed to be coming to me from out of nowhere. But I knew who it was coming from!

I had also come to full terms with the heartbreak, and the mistakes of my past. And now I understood full well who I was, and what I was meant to do with my life!

I thank *God* for allowing me to live there, and feel so close to the earth! And often as I sat on my front steps I would ponder about what I called *"The World Outside."* Meaning the so called civilized world outside the swamp, and the sad plight that it's environment had gotten into.

When *God* created the first humans, he had prepared for them a wonderfully clean, healthy, and perfect in every way planet earth to live upon. All of newly arrived mankind's needs were there for him in abundance. Every fresh water lake, stream or river flowed with pure water. The air was healthy, and the soil was alive and fertile. Mankind could not have wished for a better or more perfect earth to live upon!

Thru the centuries, as the human race progressed, all across the earth, especially during this past century, little by little the air has become more unhealthy, the water unclean, and unsafe, and in many places the soil has become infertile dust! Even the rays of the sun have become harmful to humans. Because of ignorance, and lack of foresight, almost all of the basic necessities that *God* had placed on this earth, and given to us for free, we are now often forced to purchase, and all too often at great expense!

In many areas, out of necessity we must purify all over again, the air, the water, and the soil all across the earth! Man's modern technology, the very thing that caused it all, is now the only thing that can save it! How ironic is that?

Virtually all of the environmental problems we are faced with today could have been avoided if we had been more careful and done right to begin with. Man, in his seemingly inborn and stubborn desire to make life on earth more pleasant or convenient for humans should have realized that he cannot improve on the works of *God's Creation*. We have proven beyond any doubt that all we can do is alter it, and in so many cases eventually destroy it!

If the plants and creatures of the natural world could speak, each and every one of them would ask of the human race the same thing! Stop the waste, the destruction, and the pollution all across the earth!

Even a tiny ant or single blade of grass, can show us how to cooperate with the natural plan that *God* has created for this earth!

The human race has progressed beyond all expectation and all imagination anyone ever dreamed possible! With our cell phones we can speak immediately and directly to anyone anywhere in the world. In our huge, luxurious jet airliners we can be anywhere on

"Swampwise"

earth in just a few hours! We have invented a bomb that in one explosion can destroy an entire nation in a matter of seconds! We can even fly to the moon!

We've got computers that can do almost anything. We are progressing so fast nowadays that it is all but impossible to keep up with ourselves!

One of the most startling and humbling realizations came to me in the Okefenokee Swamp! And I would caution the entire human race to be aware of this! It is a simple fact that all of our collective human knowledge, and fantastic modern technology put together cannot stop a tornado, a blizzard, the rain, or the thunder and lightning! We can't even stop a little gust of wind outside!

We can't change the time, the temperature, the phase of the moon, or the tides in the ocean. We cannot change the fact that winter follows fall, spring comes after winter. It's dark at night, and light during the day. We throw something up in the air, it comes right back down. None of these so called natural occurrences and more will ever be in the control of the human race!

No matter how far we go with our technology! No matter how smart or important we think we are, the natural laws that *God* has put in place to govern life on this planet are still, and always will be intact and in charge!

There are now probably more humans on this earth than ever before in history. That being the case, each of us, as individuals, need to be more careful every hour of every day, how we treat the life in the natural world around us. Our cooperation with the natural scheme of life on earth is more essential now than ever! How can we treat it with the respect it deserves if we do not fully understand it?

For the sake of our children, and their children to come, along with our own laws, we need to pay heed to the natural laws of nature that *God* has put in place on this planet. That, in a nutshell, is the lesson the plants and the creatures of the Okefenokee Swamp have so generously shared with me!

After eight years of self grooming, and self-education, now

known widely across the Southeast as Okefenokee Joe, it was time for me to once again to pack up, and move on. Proof that *God* had not only answered my prayers, but that he had actually spoken to me, lies in the simple fact that my life was now full of purpose! I was no longer that "wounded bear running through the woods, in terrible pain and confusion, not knowing which way to turn!"

I was Okefenokee Joe, and I was now fully prepared, and ready to move on! So, in 1981, at the age of forty-nine, feeling swampwise, and obeying a deep feeling of responsibility, I left the employ of the Okefenokee Swamp Park. Combining my new experiential swampwise knowledge, and wisdom, with my old "showbiz know-how," I once again began a new life!

For the next thirty-five years, as Okefenokee Joe, I traveled all over the Southeastern United States, sharing my message of our responsibility to, and the understanding of, the natural world around us. *God*, his Earth, and all living things upon it truly deserve our utmost respect, deep love, and genuine appreciation![1]

Now, forty years later, this book!

Note:

[1] Today, at this writing, I have changed the name of my presentation to: "Swampwise Secrets, Songs & Stories from the Land of the Trembling Earth!" I have retired the snakes! Now with my acoustic Martin Guitar, I sing the songs I have written about nature, and I tell true stories about my life in the Okefenokee, Creek and Seminole Indian history, and facts about our wild animal neighbors!

"Swampwise"

Picture courtesy of Milton Morris, 2015

The Author at the age of 83 and at the time of this writing! Still pickin' and singin', and still wearing that Thunderbird!

CHAPTER 14
SOME OF OKEFENOKEE JOE'S FAVORITE SWAMPWISE QUOTES

"Streetwise is cool, Swampwise is awesome!"

"If you don't need it, leave it!"

"It's about time someone told the snake's side of the story, and told the truth!"

"Look before you leap!"

"Snakes eat rats, not people!"

"Man cannot improve on the works of nature. Man can only alter it, and eventually destroy it."

"Sound environmentalism through education."

"Education, not legislation!"

"*God* has designed every form of life on this earth perfectly for the job he has created it to do."

"Swampwise"

"Nature does not need man! Man needs nature! And nature needs everything it has! Even things some humans do not like!"

"The next time bugs start bugging you, remember what bugs really do!"

"For every living thing in the natural world around us, "Earth day" is every day!"

"Snakes don't mean to frighten you. Snakes have more important things to do!"

"It takes teamwork to make things work! Nothing works without teamwork!"

"Hate is just a harsh word for ignorance."

"Life is impartial! Life does not care about any of us. What we do with our own life is entirely up to us.

"If I had my way I would do away with anger, jealousy, envy, greed, hate, and revenge!"

"Always seek the truth, and always speak the truth!"

"Humans are the only living things on earth that can do the understanding. Therefore it is up to us to do it!"

"I am going to absolutely ruin the bad reputation that snakes have got!"

"*God* has given us an earth to live upon. Treat it right!"

Other books written by Okefenokee Joe
Snake Hunter Snake Talk
& the Audio book Series
"Swampwise Secrets, Songs & Stories
From The Land Of The Trembling Earth!"
3 Volumes! Plus a Special Bonus CD
Visit Joe online! www.okefenokeejoe.com
Sample, Purchase, or Download his
CDs, DVDs, and Audio Books
© 2016 Okefenokee Joe Enterprises

CHAPTER 15
BACK OF THE BOOK PHOTOS

Picture courtesy of Kim Mehaffy Kilgore
- Eagle Eye Images
Okefenokee Joe;
Singer/Song Writer/Wildlife Evangelist

Picture courtesy of Bill & Linda Macky
**Okefenokee Joe/Dick Flood
Inducted into the Atlanta
Country Music Hall of Fame 2015**

"Swampwise"

Picture courtesy of Wolfgang Obst Productons
Okefenokee Joe at his Beargrass Natural History Center, Odum, Georgia, 2002

Picture courtesy of Betty Frady, 2005

OKEFENOKEE JOE'S
"Earth Day EveryDay"

Presentations;
Four Successful Decades of
Family Fun, Excitement
& Fascinating Edu-tainment!
Snakes, Secrets, Stories
& Songs From the
"Land of the Tremblin' Earth!"

1974 - 2017

SWAMPWISE
Written by

OKEFENOKEE JOE
THE END

Sample, Download, or Purchase more of

OKEFENOKEE JOE'S

Wonderful CDs, DVDs, Books, Ebooks,
and Audio Books At:
www.okefenokeejoe.com
© Copyright 2016 Okefenokee Joe Enterprises
ISBN 978-0-9973371-0-5
"SWAMPWISE"
Also Available in Ebook Form: ISBN # 978-0-9973371-6-7

www.ingramcontent.com/pod-product-compliance
Lightning Source LLC
Chambersburg PA
CBHW032043150426
43194CB00006B/399